THE
COMPLETE BOOK
OF
FREESTYLE
KARATE

THE
COMPLETE BOOK
OF
FREESTYLE
KARATE

David L. Mitchell

WARD LOCK

WARNING

Karate is a combat sport, the practice of which involves potentially dangerous technique. Readers are warned that while every effort has been made to describe techniques and their application accurately, neither the author nor the publishers can accept responsibility for injuries and accidents arising out of their practice.

AUTHOR'S APOLOGY

Owing to the absence of a suitable gender-neutral pronoun and in the interest of an easier read I have used the words 'he' and 'him' where I mean 's/he' and 'him/her'. I apologise for any irritation this may cause to female karateka.

First published in 1992 by Ward Lock

Villiers House, 41/47 Strand, London WC2N 5JE

A Cassell Imprint

© Copyright David Mitchell 1992

Photography by Martin Sellars

Cataloging in Publication Data available from the British Library

ISBN 0–7063–7053–8

Typeset by August Filmsetting, Haydock, St Helens

Printed and bound in Great Britain by
Bath Press, Bath, Avon

Caption for Page 2
Freestyle karate relies heavily upon training aides to test the effectiveness of techniques.

Caption for Page 1
Practice of Karate do or 'The Way of Karate' is intended to promote both physical and mental health.

CONTENTS

Small classes meant that there was no need to break down complex moves into their component parts.

FOREWORD

TRADITIONAL AND FREESTYLE KARATE

Many practitioners of 'traditional' karate regard freestyle karateka as the mongrels of the fraternity. They are seen as living proof of the old adage 'jack of all trades – master of none' . But in this book I will argue that it is in freestyle karate alone that the future development of this practice resides. Consider the following points.

1   The practice of karate in its present form is known to be injurious to the knee, elbow and sacroiliac joints.

2   The same practice produces performers who are expert at kicking and punching the empty air, and who often fall over or hurt themselves whenever they actually make contact with the opponent.

3   The present karate punching, kicking and striking techniques are both crude and weak by comparison with other, non-karate systems.

4   The whole theory and method of power generation and delivery of techniques is fatally flawed from the point of view of an elementary physiodynamic study. In other words, karate produces powerful-looking techniques that aren't.

5   Karate's blocks are crude and allow no transference of learning to practical use. They block techniques instead of the opponent.

6   Karate techniques have only a shallow depth of field and so are ineffective when engaging with grappling, locking, or short-range systems.

7   Karate competition does not require truly effective techniques, power or effectiveness. It degrades the martial virtues and its performance has been aptly described by one leading Japanese karate exponent as 'no more than a dance'. The press and media have described it as 'punch-up *interruptus*', where the referee's job is 'to stop the match every time it begins to get interesting'.

8   The method of teaching karate is primitive, with no national coaching qualifications. Teaching methods are authoritarian and old fashioned, resulting in a 90 per cent wastage of new students before they have completed three months training.

9   Worst of all, karate is now taught without an attendant philosophy. Students are taught to be masters of karate technique, rather than masters of karate itself. Cowardly novice grades become bullying black belts, and so forth.

Let's begin by looking into the detail behind some of these claims. The first is that 'traditional' karate is somehow better than freestyle because the former is rooted in martial history. But, as we shall see from the first chapter of this book, those who have researched karate's disappointingly thin reliable history have shown that the art as practised today has been in existence only since the early years of the twentieth century. If the history is to be believed, then the only way you can apply 'traditional' to 'karate' is to accept that when it is used in this particular sense, 'traditional' doesn't mean very old. So to avoid perpetuating the myth of 'traditional' karate, I will henceforth use the expression 'classical' karate.

A second misconception is that classical karate embodies some kinds of metaphysical principles and/or moral virtues which are not present in freestyle. But just what these mysterious and exclusive concepts are is difficult to identify. And further, what physical evidence do we have for the existence of these principles and virtues, apart from high-sounding words? It is certainly true that we cannot see or weigh a principle – though we can look for evidence of it in the behaviour and demeanour of those who are said to possess it. As we shall see, our searches go largely unrewarded.

To my mind, freestyle karate is free of all this hypocrisy. It makes no spurious claims to a martial history and neither does it profess to hold high-sounding virtues.

Perhaps classical karate can lay claim to a greater tradition of skill? The evidence is to the contrary and in the following paragraphs I will try to highlight some of classical karate's most serious and obvious shortcomings.

From a purely ethno-historical perspective, there seems to be good evidence for believing that by and large, the best Chinese martial art teachers never taught the core principles of their practice to everybody and anybody – least of all to foreigners. So I very much doubt whether the Okinawan fathers of karate received these principles from their Chinese teachers. I further doubt whether, in turn, the Okinawans taught all their secrets to the Japanese. And it is my own personal experience that the Japanese never gave away all their advantages to the bigger gaijin. If you have managed to follow this, then you must join me in suspecting that the karate we Westerners now practise is several crucial steps removed from those original systems which contributed towards its development.

We can gain some support for this theory by looking first at karate's blocking techniques.

These simply cannot be compared with those shown by authentic Chinese systems. With the exception of two techniques from the Wado ryu syllabus (which, incidentally, are taken from jiu-jitsu), karate blocks all deflect attacking techniques. Yet if you block a technique, then the opponent is at least theoretically able to throw another at you. But if you take a leaf from such as Wing Chun Kuen and block the opponent instead, you prevent him from launching any more techniques without a radical rearrangement of stance and guard. So, advanced Chinese blocks not only prevent the opponent's techniques from reaching you, they also close him off, leaving him helpless.

I want next to refer again to the shallow depth of field over which karate techniques are effective. Two karateka fight most comfortably when their leading guard hands are about a fist's width apart. Close inside this range and your opponent will either back off or immediately attack you. This is no accident! It happens because karate punches, strikes and kicks are almost all medium-range techniques. Close the distance and technique effectiveness drops sharply.

To be sure, karate does teach a small number of short-range techniques – knee, elbow and close punch, for example – but these are not practised to the same extent as other techniques and, in any case, they are quite limited in their application.

Kicking techniques can only be used when the opponent is at middle or long distance. Close inside that range and they become a liability. Count the number of times you see a score awarded when the opponent counter-punches a kick. I realise that competition is an artificial activity, but it is nevertheless relevant in what it shows in this instance.

Also, consider the way in which some classical karate kicks place the user at a greater than necessary disadvantage. There is no denying that back kick is a powerful technique. But under what circumstances can you safely turn your back on the opponent and then stand on one leg?

Karate's 'corkscrew' punch doesn't work if you have to punch at the face of a taller opponent. The middle joints of your fingers connect – not the knuckles. This is why some karateka rotate their fists only part-way when punching upwards.

Is it sensible to train for a powerful punch without first preparing the knuckles and wrist for the impact such a punch will generate? Why, then, do so few classical karate schools insist upon proper fist preparation?

Karate's method of power development requires specialised stances and body movements which inevitably restrict technique application. For example, the so-called 'pulley principle' requires karateka to use hips, shoulders and centre of gravity in a complex series of co-ordinated movements. If this is the only way by which karate develops power, then are we saying that it is not possible to punch effectively when we are seated or prone? These situations don't happen often in the training hall – but that is only because everyone has agreed to certain protocols. And these protocols do not operate out in the street!

The fact is that sometimes even the most skilled martial artists fall to the floor or are thrown during sparring practice. Yet classical karate does not teach prone defence. And what happens if the karateka wants to restrain the opponent, rather than knock him out? Classical karate does not teach restraining techniques either.

You may, of course, legitimately defend classical karate by claiming that teaching a comprehensive and effective fighting system is not the object of practice. If this is the case, then all well and good – my criticisms can gain no purchase. But having said that, I think that few karateka would actually be prepared to admit that classical karate

is, to some extent at least, ineffective as a fighting system.

Freestyle karate builds on the classical base, using mid-range techniques when appropriate – otherwise training to develop independent power, so techniques are effective regardless of stance. When the opponent closes range, the freestyle karateka is not limited to backing off in order to remain effective. Instead, he can use short-range techniques to strike hard even from close distances. If the opponent closes yet further, then a short punch combined with an effective throw will conclude matters satisfactorily. In addition, the freestyle karateka is taught practical and effective restraining techniques such as are used by police forces in Britain.

In conclusion then, what I have tried to argue is that there are no grounds whatsoever for regarding classical karate as in any way superior to a freestyle system that is properly put together. In fact, it is difficult to avoid the conclusion that the freestyle system is actually better – if only in terms of its wider applicability.

However, no fighting system exists independently of the people who practise it. So it is impossible to compare the systems *per se* – only the people who practise them. Therefore, we can only ever know whether one karateka is better than another. And I have more than a fleeting suspicion that many so-called classical karateka are good in spite of the system they study.

1

A SHORT HISTORY OF KARATE AND ITS DEVELOPMENT

THE EVIDENCE FOR TRADITIONAL KARATE

Many people believe in the existence of what they call 'traditional karate'; yet karate as we know it today is actually less than fifty years old. Others say that karate began way back in the mid eighteenth century. If it did, then not only was it not called 'karate' then, but it didn't look like it either!

As far as we can tell, karate developed out of an Okinawan fighting system called *to-de* and this in turn may be predated by an earlier form, known simply as *te*. *To-de* might have been an umbrella name for what in fact was a range of quite unrelated fighting systems devised by farmers and peasants.

THE BEGINNINGS OF KARATE IN OKINAWA

Okinawa is the largest of the Ryukyu Islands which stretch like stepping-stones between the south-west tip of Japan and the southern Chinese mainland. Its position, therefore, puts it within the spheres of influence of both those powerful nations.

Fourteenth-century Okinawa was divided into three kingdoms – Nanzan in the south, Chuzan in the centre and Hokuzan in the north. In 1372, the king of Chuzan formed an alliance with China and, as a consequence, a party of thirty-six Chinese families came to Okinawa and settled in the village of Toei.

Chuzan's alliance with China was uninterrupted when, in 1429, the three kingdoms were united by King Sho Hashi. He was succeeded by King Sho Shin, who imposed a ban both on the wearing of swords and on the ownership of private armories. Thereafter, martial art practice went into a decline that lasted some 180 years. In February 1609, Okinawa was invaded by a force of 3,000 warriors belonging to the Satsuma clan of mainland Japan. Again, this did not affect Okinawa's relationship with China.

In 1661 the Chinese sent military attaché Kosokun (the Okinawan reading of his Chinese name) to Okinawa. Kosokun was a renowned martial arts master who is believed to have taught Sakugawa Satunushi and Yari Kitan. 'Karate'* Sakugawa, as he was known, was already a famous exponent of Okinawan martial art and is said to have combined the two systems together to form the basis of what later came to be called *shuri te* ('hand of Shuri').

Kosokun was not the only visiting teacher. Chinto, Waishinzan, Iwah and Ason are also reported to have taught Okinawans at Toei. Okinawan martial artists also travelled to the Chinese mainland to train and Yari Chatan, the grandson of

---

Kicks to targets above the waist are not a feature of early classical karate – they came in much later.

*'Karate' here means 'China hand', not the 'empty hand' of modern karate.

Yari Kitan, spent 20 years there learning southern Shaolin kung fu.

We can identify three quite different threads of development in the fighting arts during the period of Okinawa's annexation.

First, schools of covert weaponry arose among farmers and peasants using quarterstaffs, sickles, rice flails, rice grinder handles and short tridents. Such schools appear to owe little to Chinese influences.

Farmers and peasants were fairly tough and the system they devised was characterised more by strength than finesse. There were as many schools as there were families, and all practised basic techniques and free sparring. Training kata did not put in an appearance until very much later. Some remnants of this early thread can still be seen today in *ryukyu kobudo*. A rudimentary form of unarmed combat also developed as a secondary system and this, too, owed little to direct Chinese influence.

The second thread of karate development arose among more privileged classes of Okinawan society. Young nobles and members of the merchant class probably knew little if anything about the peasant fighting system, drawing instead on Chinese instruction at Toei and on the mainland.

The third thread of development arose from various combinations of Chinese and Okinawan practices. This thread is, I suspect, the true founder of karate as we now know it.

THE SPREAD OF KARATE IN OKINAWA

The three principal towns of Okinawa each developed a slightly different expression of early karate. That of the capital, Shuri, became known as *shuri-te*. This was characterised by light, agile movements and its founder is said to be Sakugawa Satunushi. *Naha-te* is thought to have originated in the city of Naha. It is characterised by strong stances and circular movements, and its founder is said to be Higaonna Kannryo. *Tomari-te* first appeared in the Tomari area and it combined the features of both *shuri-te* and *naha-te*. The styles expanded, overlapped and the distinctions between them blurred: *naha-te* and *tomari-te* merging to form *shorei-ryu* and *shuri-te* to *shorin ryu*.

Towards the end of the nineteenth century, the leading Okinawan masters banded together to found an umbrella liaison and development organisation known as the Shobukai. One of the Shobukai's decisions was to name the Okinawan fighting art *karate* ('China hand') as a tribute to the early Chinese teachers.

Karate eventually became known to the Japanese who, as a result of changes in policy, began to encourage its practice as a means of instilling martial virtue in the Okinawans. This objective assumed particular importance during 1898 when the Japanese imposed military conscription on the islanders.

FUNAKOSHI GICHIN – THE FATHER OF MODERN KARATE

The Chairman of the Okinawan Shobukai was the schoolteacher Funakoshi Gichin. He was responsible for much of the initial promotion of karate, giving displays for the Japanese Navy and, in 1917, demonstrating karate before Hirohito, the then crown prince. However, despite those few brief but memorable occasions, karate lapsed into almost total obscurity. Its conspicuous lack of progress is reflected in the fact that Funakoshi was unable to support himself as a karate teacher and had to work as a part-time janitor.

But a turning point came when Funakoshi met Kano Jigoro, the founder of judo. He was greatly impressed by the way Kano had remodelled jiujitsu to give prominence to its scientific principles and health-promoting practice. Thereafter, Funakoshi began to stress those same principles in karate and, in an effort to make the art more acceptable to mainlanders, he changed its name to 'way of the empty hand'. Though the title 'karate' was retained, its Japanese characters were changed to fit the new meaning.

THE KARATE RYU

By the early twentieth century, several different schools of karate sought to align themselves with traditional Japanese martial art practice by adopting the *ryu*-system. For our purposes, *'ryu'* can be translated as 'school', meaning a core of practice extending back to the founder.

In classical Japanese and Chinese martial arts, the founder typically inaugurated the school following a mystical revelation of some kind. This revelation gave new insights into practice, and inspired the founder to adopt and refine new principles. These subsequently became the core teachings of that *ryu*.

Founders took great care to ensure that core teachings were passed only to those who were thought capable of receiving them and the mandate for interpreting them passed from hand to hand down the generations to the present day.

Occasionally, senior students interpreted the core teachings in a highly individualistic way. Sometimes they introduced changes arising out of new insights, or they merely customised some movements, the better to suit a particular build or temperament. However, when these interpretations varied too greatly from accepted tradition, the innovators were obliged to leave and found another *ryu*.

Four major *ryu* were recognised by the governing Japanese Karate Federation. These were the *shotokan*, the *wado kai*, the *shito kai* and the *goju kai*. In addition, there is always at least one umbrella group to take the lesser *ryu* into membership.

HOW SOCIAL CHANGES ALTERED THE NATURE OF KARATE PRACTICE

As a result of annexation, for a time Okinawans were forbidden by law from engaging in any martial-type activity that might make them more difficult to govern. But human nature being what it is, if you want to encourage people to do something, simply pass a law against doing it! The Okinawans responded by training secretly.

For something to remain a secret, it must be shared by very few people – so an undercover karate teacher would not advertise for new members in the local newspaper. Instead, he would train only the members of his own family, and perhaps a handful of close friends and their immediate family. For if the student lacked close kin-

ship or friendship loyalties, he would not have the same incentive to remain silent under duress.

Sensible teachers therefore denied that they practised martial art because each new student meant not so much a larger rice bowl as an ever-increasing likelihood of being denounced to the authorities. Thus, I think we can safely surmise that classes were small.

Training took place behind closed doors, or in the countryside. Sometimes sessions were held at night in dimly lit courtyards, but always there was a danger of discovery. The Tokugawa authorities were not known for presuming anyone innocent until proven guilty and suspicion alone was often quite enough to result in someone's arrest and execution. It is important to stress this aspect, since it is so far from our own experience of training.

The possibility of local militia suddenly bursting in on a session had to be taken into account. For instance, such a possibility ruled out the wearing of conspicuous training uniforms and coloured sashes, so students trained in their everyday clothes.

It was also impossible to have an undisguised punching post or wooden man standing in the garden. Presumably, trees would have been used instead and the pads of rice straw hanging from the wall could be just pillows put out to air. And what might the young people be doing? Perhaps enjoying a spot of tomfoolery – a little wrestling. You know how young people are, officer! Or perhaps they were practising an old Okinawan dance – indeed, some kata were disguised to look like dances precisely for this reason.

Class size determines the method of teaching. In a small class, everyone stands fairly close to the teacher and can easily follow his movements as he performs a series of techniques. There is no need to break that series down into its component parts and it is not essential, even, that each and every technique has a name. The teacher simply repeats the whole sequence in silence, until students pick up the correct movements.

Teaching occurred through self-revelation in which the students themselves discovered why they were performing a certain technique in a certain way. The master provided no explanation. Compare this with modern coaching methods where everything is explained and little is left to discover.

After training, everyone retired to the living room for a meal and to discuss the significance and context of what had been taught. Everything was revealed, and nothing held back.

Then social circumstances began to change. The prohibition on training was eased and suddenly the Japanese actually wanted the Okinawans to practise. The Imperial Army was being made larger and needed conscripts who were fit, eager and ready to fight effectively for emperor and country.

For the first time, classes grew larger and soon not all the students could hear or see what the teacher was showing them. Long series of unnamed movements might well have caused problems, so each technique was named and sequences were broken up into their individual components. Henceforth, a single sequence would be taught as separate techniques to the count of *ichi-ni-san* and through this, what once was a flowing and seamless movement developed a sort of stutter – like the flicker that one sees in old films. Karateka began to think in terms of single movements instead of sequences.

Readers should not dismiss this assertion lightly by saying 'So what?', because it has had the most serious effect upon karate practice. The joins between movements remain, even when each technique has been learned perfectly. No matter how advanced he may be, a student trained in this manner must inevitably think in terms of 'first block, then punch'.

Nevertheless, this new method made it possible to teach karate to large numbers and, emboldened by its success, teachers made up a series of elementary *kata* for novices to learn. These were symmetrical and, again, could be performed to a count. Rows of young people moving in perfect unison must have stirred onlookers to admiration then, as they still do now.

This aesthetic consideration was important because karate was competing for popularity with judo and kendo, and it suffered from three very serious disadvantages. First, it was not what could be described as a brand leader. Both judo and kendo had conditioned the public to see martial art as a strictly regimented and orderly activity, so

karate was obliged to follow suit. Secondly, karate originated on Okinawa, which the mainlanders regarded as a rural backwater peopled by bumpkins. Thirdly, karate's ambassador to Japan was a mere schoolteacher and not someone from a martial arts family!

But on the credit side, karate was new and offered something a little out of the ordinary. Those who took part in Kendo used bamboo swords and judo looked like a form of wrestling, so karate filled the boxing niche. This meant playing down its own grappling techniques in favour of powerful looking punches and kicks.

Other fundamental changes were involved in promoting karate. Though effective, the old karate was relatively uninteresting to look at. For while training to seize an opponent by his testicles may be effective, it is not aesthetically pleasing to the spectator! Also, Funakoshi favoured only short, thrusting kicks to the opponent's instep, shin, knees and groin. Again, though effective, these were not spectacular as the high, circling kicks practised in Japanese-dominated Korea. And with the incorporation of these into the karate syllabus, its previously close engagement distance was extended, causing a knock-on effect in the areas of technique, usage and application.

Mainland Japanese embraced Funakoshi's remodelled karate, and it came to set the standards for other schools to follow. After the Second World War, 'neo-karate' spread worldwide and became the accepted norm, while Okinawa, the home of karate, became a martial backwater.

COMMERCIALISM AND LEISURE KARATE

A major factor affecting the development of karate was commercialism. During the 1960s it became possible to earn a good living from teaching the art. Students began to be a source of substantial revenue and, in an atmosphere of increasing competition, ethical and technical standards of practice began to decline.

The era of the professional instructor coincides with the phenomenon of the leisure karateka. This is a person who practises for a few hours of pleasure each week. But karate is not something you can learn in two lessons a week – it should be a way of life. So if the professional instructor wants to maintain his lifestyle, then accommodations have to be made in what he is teaching.

Small wonder then, that karate should have undergone some pretty fundamental changes in the last forty years.

KARATE COMPETITION

A third major contribution to karate's recent development has been made through the promotion of competition. As early as the 1920s, students wanted to test themselves against others by means of a competition – but Funakoshi wouldn't allow it. He was clearly aware of the way competition could change the very nature of karate.

Competition prohibited some effective techniques on the grounds that they were dangerous. It fostered the use of weakened techniques, imposed rules and created an ego-dominated activity where the emphasis is on winning.

In spite of these criticisms, competition is now the major public manifestation of karate practice and if you have never won a major competition, then your karate will be regarded by many as suspect.

FREESTYLE KARATE

Freestyle karate began in America during the 1960s when shortcomings in the classical system were first picked up on. In America the multi-discipline tournament, at which classical karate students fought competitors from kung fu, tang soo do and taekwondo, was pioneered.

You see, sparring within one school does not broaden your horizons because opponents use the same syllabus as you do. This is why Chinese teachers sent their students to train at other schools. For a time, classical karate ryu did the same thing, until increasing competition eventually put paid to the practice.

In this book, classical karate techniques have been taken back to their origins – when they were still effective in a fighting environment. To them have been added the short-range power and techniques of Shaolin kung fu, the sophisticated kicks of taekwondo, the grappling techniques of aikido and the throws of judo.

The point about freestyle is that it does not have a rigid structure. Although primarily a striking system, you can emphasise either mid or short range techniques – the choice is yours. Also, the number of grappling and throwing techniques can be expanded or reduced to suit individual preference, so there is ample room for individual customisation.

Unfettered by rigid adherence to narrow dogma, the freestyle karateka has at least the possibility to develop a truly effective fighting art, using all the modern physiological and psychological training methods available. In my view, freestyle represents the only avenue of future development open to a karate which has now otherwise ossified.

2

A PHILOSOPHY OF KARATE PRACTICE

INTRODUCTION

Many karateka look askance at the thought of philosophy, primarily, I suppose, because of the confusing Eastern terminology that attaches to it. As a result, there is a tendency nowadays to concentrate on technique. But technique without philosophy is like computer hardware without its operating software. The karateka must have a philosophy of practice, because without it, he will never be truly effective. This chapter is therefore intended to help us to understand the role played by philosophy in karate practice.

Let's begin by looking at two examples. The first is that of the karateka who has trained until his technique is unbeatable. He enters a competition but is eliminated in the first round by someone who is nowhere near as technically accomplished. We would all agree that this is possible. The second example is that of the slight female who is attacked by two strong young men and puts them both to flight. What conclusions can we draw from these examples?

First, they show that skill or training in the execution of technique does not guarantee the necessary mental resolve to apply it. Secondly, a person can possess the necessary resolve without having any sort of training at all. This does not, of course, mean that skill is of no value, though perhaps we in the West place too much reliance on technique and too little on the mind that operates that technique. Whatever you may think, it does remain a fact that today's karate training consists, in the main, of teaching technique only.

Many karate schools are aware that someone who performs well in normal circumstances may not do so well when stressed. This is why some of them practise *shugyo*, or 'austere training'. Shugyo involves both intense physical and mental training.

There is no doubt that hard training does concentrate those of a determined nature simply by sieving out the dilettantes. But does determination to train hard also make you resolute when facing a real opponent? Like skill, hard physical training is no disadvantage – but again, I don't think that it provides the whole answer.

Some karate schools practise very realistic sparring in which injury of some sort is almost inevitable. This may well inure karateka to levels of injury and challenge, though a gap still remains between the real and the simulated. It is this gap which can still give rise to failure.

It is a well-known fact that the body adapts itself to training in a highly specific way. Indeed, it is so specific that you can train to a peak in one area of fitness, and still leave your body wholly deficient in others. Perhaps mental training operates in the same way. Perhaps we can become resolute at training hard, or at sustaining sparring injuries while still being unable to defeat a real-life opponent.

Technique without the attendant martial mind is like computer hardware without the operating software.

ANXIETY

If I asked you to walk along a plank lying flat on the floor, you would do so with ease. But if I supported it by its ends, 200 ft above the ground, what then? It still has the same width and length, so why are you now apprehensive about walking across it? Obviously the answer must lie in the consequences of making a mistake. When the plank lies on the floor, the consequences of a mistake need not even be considered. But lift it up . . .

So, to train you to cross the plank, I might lift it from the floor in gradual increments. It might take a lot of time but, eventually, you would gain the confidence required and feel able to cross it at any height.

It is difficult to define actually what anxiety is, but since we have all felt it at some time or another, we know well enough what the term means. For our purposes, we can regard it as a mental state in which we see a gap between what we think is being asked of us and what we think we are capable of supplying. If we are forced by circumstances to try and cross a gap which appears to us to be unbridgeable, then we undergo a sort of mental collapse and run away.

However, what we may be asked to do is not really outside our capabilities – we only think it is. Like the plank lying on the floor, we can walk across it easily. However, the outcome of a competition may be all-important, so it is as though the plank has suddenly been lifted up very high. If we become too anxious, then we are almost certain to lose. So what we need to know is how it might be possible to reduce our anxiety to a level where it is merely helpful in making us fully alert.

THE IMPORTANCE OF A MARTIAL PHILOSOPHY

While it is perhaps understandable that we Westerners came to attribute superhuman feats of fighting ability to the Japanese, it is nevertheless a fact that the arts themselves were of minor importance when compared with the power of the Japanese philosophy. This misunderstanding persists to the present day, with the result that millions of people, in more than a hundred countries, are all practising martial art techniques which they hope will make them into fearless and invincible warriors.

But what is this philosophy, this understanding that enables us to use our martial skills to the best effect? In the first instance, it derives in part from a society which placed little value on the life of the individuals, except in so far as that life served the interests of that particular society. In the second instance, it was in part based on the observance of a life-denying philosophy like Buddhism. But since we cannot all arrange to be born Japanese, then we must look for another option to see whether it might be possible to loosen anxiety's hold over us.

Even if we find such a way, I doubt whether we could ever reach a state of mind not uncommon to many Japanese as late as 1945, in which life or death means nothing; and even assuming that goal were possible, I'm not sure it fits in very well with the requirements of modern western society.

Instead, we might set the aim of reducing our fear and anxiety as our goal, instead of abolishing it altogether. So let's begin by reviewing our specific aims in this respect.

THE AIMS OF A MARTIAL PHILOSOPHY

First of all, we must be able to get ourselves into the correct frame of mind before engaging in combat. We may face a truly formidable opponent, in which case our initial aim must now be to avoid losing the fight before we exchange our opening techniques. Secondly, we must be able to fight with a mind unclouded by the fear of failure. Such a fear inhibits skill, causing us to miss opportunities which, under less stressed circumstances, we would have jumped at. We think: 'He can't really have lifted his front guarding hand that high, unless he actually wants me to go under it!' And while we agonise, the gap closes and the opponent attacks.

Thirdly, even while responding to the opponent on a physical level, we must be able to see him as someone for whom we feel no anger or fear. We must see defeating him simply as incidental, for the main purpose is now that of defeating ourselves. In this connection, consider the saying of the swordmaster Yagyu Shinkage (1571–1646): 'I do not know how to defeat others. I only know how to win over myself.'

This clearly shows the importance of controlling one's own fears and anxieties, so the mind is left calm and the body unfettered. Such control must lead to the purest expression of skill that we are capable of attaining.

Some karateka are aggressive rather than anxious and regard this as a frame of mind to encourage. This should not be so! As a matter of fact, being aggressive is as bad as being over-anxious. Aggression is another expression of emotion and emotion can inhibit true skill!

MEDITATION – A PRACTICAL EXPRESSION OF MARTIAL PHILOSOPHY

The tranquil state of mind in which you are neither anxious nor angry, yet remain capable of supreme skill, is a curious one. Known in Buddhism as the state of 'no self', it does not occur naturally and can only be developed by the appropriate training. Unfortunately, this training is beyond the reach of the average person with the average commitments of time and money. However, it is still possible to make a worthwhile attempt by aiming at the cultivation of a sort of minimal no self. This is achieved through meditation.

So, first of all, what exactly is meditation? Perhaps the best way to think of it is by considering what it does. It acts as a psychic tool which allows us to gain an insight into ourselves; ultimately to recognise that what we consider as 'I' is no more than a changing collection of cravings, desires and anxieties. By means of meditation, we become able to see these feelings from a detached viewpoint, as though we were standing outside of ourselves. We see fears and anxieties arising, but it is as though they are separate from us.

In essence, meditation involves withdrawing from emotions and thoughts, either by blanking them out, or by simply sitting back and observing them, as though they were not part of us. The latter is the most suitable form of meditation for martial artists. But, whichever method you select, the object remains the same – to achieve mental tranquillity combined with alertness.

Studies by psychologists have shown that meditation gives rise to a form of consciousness similar to that which we encounter during deep relaxation. Electroencephalograms (EEGs) of meditating subjects reveal brain activity like that normally associated with sleep, interspersed with signals characteristic of alert attention.

Meditating subjects respond quite differently to stimuli when compared to non-meditating controls. Though relaxed, the meditating subject is highly receptive to stimuli and, further, this receptivity does not diminish over a period of stimulation. It is as though our mind has become more open and less inclined to filter out repeating stimuli. We could regard this as a form of increased alertness.

It is a common misapprehension that meditation allows the body to act completely of its own volition. Consider the case where you drive home by the same route each evening and one night you are very tired. You arrive on your doorstep without any recollection of having driven your car there. Here it appears that the body has been doing all the mechanical actions concerned with driving – changing gear, steering etc. – seemingly without any supervision by the higher brain centres.

However, a part of the brain is always involved in your actions. It is just that the level of attention has dropped and only enough is left 'on line' to get you through an uneventful drive. However, were an emergency to occur, then you would lose valuable instants in bringing your brain back fully on line. Since martial combat is more like an eventful drive, then it follows that we cannot simply train our bodies to react on autopilot, as it were.

Yes, we can get by on a small number of reflex actions, but a certain level of mental involvement remains absolutely essential. So what precisely is that involvement? It appears to be the intellect minus the emotions – the fears, the anxieties, the worries. This is the stage we must attain in order to achieve our objectives.

One Eastern theory about meditation claims that the normally active mind consumes a great amount of energy in producing so many thoughts. When mental activity is stilled by meditation, surplus energy then becomes available for other purposes – which, we are told, include such things as improvements in health. Interesting though this theory is, there is no physical evidence to back it up. However, it is certainly the case that what we might call a 'tranquil' state is related to a very slight reduction in brain metabolism.

Another Eastern theory is that thought energy belongs to the kind known as *yang*. This is characterised by being active, hot and dry. Its opposite is the *yin* kind which is characterised by being passive, cold and wet. Daoists therefore recommend banishing one's yang thoughts by concentrating upon a yin image, and one of the most popular is to envisage yourself floating in cool, dark water. Imagine you can feel the currents drifting over you. Feel the wetness against your skin.

Such a powerful visualisation is certainly effective in suppressing thought, but whether that is so because of the principles of yin and yang is another matter. My own opinion is that any powerful and restful visualisation is likely to be just as effective.

PROGRESSIVE MUSCULAR RELAXATION

Simple physical drills to lower anxiety do not seem to be as effective as meditation. Progressive muscular relaxation ('PMR') is a therapy sometimes used to calm athletes before they perform. It involves taking up a comfortable position and then imagining that your muscles are going to sleep. First of all you make your feet and ankles relax, then your calves, and so on to the thighs etc. By the time you get to your head, the idea is that you should be quite relaxed. Indeed, there are some reports of people who have practised PMR so successfully that they dropped off to sleep.

This shows up an interesting difference between PMR and meditation. The latter calms the mind but leaves it alert. The former calms the mind and can send you to sleep! Further, a stimulus given during PMR therapy is either ignored, or it returns you immediately to a full state of alertness – aggression, anxieties and all! PMR clearly has some advantages over other forms of relaxation but it may not be so useful for karate.

PRACTISING MEDITATION

Despite the shortcomings of PMR for our purposes we can still regard it as a form of what we might call 'concentrative meditation', where the field of awareness is narrowed down to a small area – in this case making successive muscle groups relax. An alternative is to select a word you like the sound of, repeating it softly each time you breathe out. As you become more skilled, you can repeat your word silently, listening to its sound in your mind.

This is one of the easiest introductions to meditation and it is the one I recommend for anyone meditating for the first time. It can be practised while travelling on the train or the bus (but not while driving the car!), but you can't use it in situations where mental alertness is required, so like PMR, it has only a limited application to karate practice. Nevertheless, do not neglect it because the mental discipline it requires is a good preparation for more suitable forms of meditation.

To practise a more suitable type of meditation, sit comfortably with your back upright and your hands lying naturally in your lap. Gently press the tip of your tongue behind your upper front teeth and breathe regularly, using the diaphragm rather than your rib-cage. If you manage this, you will find that your chest hardly moves.

Rest your eyes on whatever takes your fancy and just sit absolutely still. Don't try to blank your thoughts out at all, just let them wander about, but don't encourage them in any way. Now is not the time to become interested in a particular line of thought; just let it go. This is very difficult to do at first. In fact it is almost impossible not to become attached to an interesting line of thought, but every second you delay this from happening is an advancement.

If you are worried that your progress is slow, think about weight training for a moment. The first time you try to lift a heavy weight, you succeed in moving it perhaps by an inch. But if you keep trying, then you will eventually succeed in pressing it above your head. It is the same with meditation, which is difficult at first but becomes easier with practice. Eventually you will be able to meditate while doing other things such as practising kata. You are not focusing down your attention – it is just that you don't become attached to your thoughts and the fears that accompany them. Your mind is attentive to what you are doing, but there is no conflict between mind and body; no fear or anxiety. The alert yet calm mind sees what is there and the body acts accordingly – not in the blind manner of a conditioned reflex.

DYNAMIC MEDITATION

The next stage in the meditation programme is to be able to meditate while training. This will take a little longer, so maintain your static training at its present level as you begin dynamic training.

To be able to meditate while performing karate requires that you know the technique or *kata*. If you have to stop and think which move follows what, then your thoughts are no longer unattached and you will return to the world of anxiety and fear. So the first essential prerequisite of dynamic meditation is to know the physical expression of the technique, so you can perform it without conscious thought. This requires skill, and skill, in its turn, requires practice.

PUTTING MEDITATION INTO THE SCHEME OF PRACTICE

Practising the techniques of karate without a martial philosophy leads to the failures we see all around us in modern karate training. We know what the objects of such a philosophy are, and we know how to use meditation as a way of helping us to follow that philosophy. It therefore remains only to practise meditation.

Begin with concentrative static meditation and try to spend at least 10 minutes a day practising it. Extend this as far as you are able aiming eventually to reach a limit of 90 minutes. When you have the hang of it, also begin meditating without fixing your thoughts on any one thing, i.e. unconcentrative meditation. As you become more proficient, you can gradually and commensurately reduce the amount of time spent in concentrative meditation until eventually you can sustain 90 minutes of the unconcentrated type.

Practise your physical training at the same time so you eventually arrive at a point where your physical skill at technique performance equals your mental skill at meditation. And when these two halves are brought together, you will have turned yourself into the most perfect expression of skill that you, as an individual, are capable of.

A final word before beginning meditation practice: approach it in the correct frame of mind. Excessive solemnity is inappropriate, as is hilarity. Simply be natural and avoid meditating when you are emotional, sleepy, when you have been drinking, or after a heavy meal.

HOW TO KNOW IF YOUR MARTIAL PHILOSOPHY IS DEVELOPING

When you first practise a roundhouse kick to the head, your technique feels awkward and looks unskilled. But after you have practised for a while, the technique begins both to feel and look good. These are the markers which tell you when you are getting your training right. So are there similar markers for your mental training?

The answer to this is 'Yes'!

If your meditation programme is working, you will find yourself becoming more relaxed during training and less anxious about such things as sparring. You may also find that you are less aggressive in the world outside the training hall, no longer taking offence and losing your temper. So the correct mental training will cause your martial philosophy to overspill into everyday life and you will come to live the way of martial art. Only then can you describe yourself accurately as 'a martial artist'.

But, finally, a word of caution: your mental programme will take at least as long as your physical training; significant effects will not begin to appear until quite late in practice. So don't be dispirited if, at a junior grade, you can control your body and perform techniques well but can't yet control your anxiety. On the other hand, if you are a black belt and still experience aggression/fear, then something has gone seriously wrong with half of your training!

3

GETTING THE BEST FROM KARATE TRAINING

INTRODUCTION

Practising good karate means performing techniques with skill – but how is this skill acquired? First, it is acquired through comparing your technique to a template (i.e. the instructor). How skilled you are will be reflected in how closely your performance matches that of the template. Secondly, skill acquisition is related to the number of times you practise a technique. In general terms, the more you practise, the more your body learns what is required of it. So, if you can manage only three repetitions before becoming exhausted, then it will take you longer to acquire the skill than if you could manage, say, six repetitions. Thus, improving your stamina will ultimately improve your skill.

Next to skill, speed is perhaps the most important element of fitness to the karateka. You must be able to advance quickly to outpace the opponent, or to retreat speedily from the path of an incoming technique. Secondly, you must be able to deliver a kick or punch so fast that the opponent has no time to avoid it. So, delivering a skilled karate technique requires speed.

Ultimately, however, there comes a time when speed of muscle contraction reaches its maximum for any individual. When that ceiling is reached, further gains in impact force can only be made by increasing the strength of muscle contraction. So strength drills must be built into the skilled karateka's training programme too.

A lightly-built person has an inherent mass disadvantage over a larger-framed opponent. This can be at least partly remedied in two ways. The first is by means of a strength training programme which adds muscle bulk, and one of the most effective ways of achieving this is through weight training. The second is to add a dynamic component to karate technique. Body mass is not increased as such, though by moving it in a certain way, it can be made to seem more substantial. This method is covered during descriptions of technique application.

Skilled karate techniques use all the body's abilities to bend, stretch and reach in a way that doesn't damage muscles and ligaments. So suppleness and mobility must also be added to our training programme.

We can say that skilled karate techniques require us to have what we might call four 'S' factors. We will now look at these in more detail, and see how each can be acquired.

MORE ABOUT THE 'S' FACTORS

Strength

Muscles can be made to work against each other without causing joint movement. This is isometric strength. Try it out by interlocking your fingers in front of your stomach, then trying to pull your hands apart. If you grip tightly enough, the muscles of your shoulders will bulge, but no movement occurs at the shoulder and elbow joints. Unfortunately, isometric strength training produces only a restricted kind of strength which are relaxed . . . Also, it is difficult to move quickly when all your muscles are fighting against each other. The trick, therefore, is to tense the muscles only when it is necessary to do so, relaxing them immediately afterwards. This sharp isometric contraction is an important part of karate training and we shall encounter it many times during practice.

A different form of strength training makes the muscle work through moving a joint. Highlight a specific action you want to strengthen and then progressively overload the operating muscles with bodyweight or free weights so they are forced to contract more strongly. However, the muscle must always be able to produce movement against the applied loading because that is what distinguishes isotonic muscle training from isometric.

Fig 1 **Some forms of classical karate training pit one muscle against another.**

is related to the length of the muscle under contraction. So get the maximum benefit from isometric training by varying the angle of your joints through which the muscles are acting.

Another drawback with isometric training is that the contracted muscles press upon the blood vessels they enclose, causing a marked rise in blood pressure. This factor may be important to older karateka.

Classical karate uses many isometric drills. For example, the kata sanchin pits one group of muscles against another until the whole body becomes rigid (Fig 1). The low stances of some classical styles build isometric strength in the locating muscles of the knee joint (Fig 2). Since the knee joint commonly suffers from karate training, then it follows that any form of protection is helpful.

While isometric body training certainly does make the body rigid and capable of withstanding heavy blows, the muscles cannot constantly be kept in a state of contraction – they must relax at some time or other. And a blow struck while they

Fig 2 **Low stances are thought to increase the strength of upper leg muscles, with consequent benefits for the knee joint.**

Speed

Decide whether you want to achieve absolute maximum speed, or what we might call 'optimum' speed. This is the fastest a technique can travel at and still develop power. This latter option is more relevant to practical karate, though not to competition karate.

To explain the difference between these two kinds of speed, consider a kick. It is possible to kick with a whiplash action of the lower leg that snaps the foot out and back in a blur of movement, though such a kick develops a relatively low impact. Alternatively, you can swivel the supporting leg and thrust the kicking hip forward in a slower action that develops more impact. Here, the optimum to aim for is a good compromise between speed and impact.

The limiting factors affecting speed are as follows:

1 Muscle fibre type. Speed of muscle contraction is affected by the percentage of fast-twitch fibres a muscle contains. Some karateka have more fast-twitch fibres than others, so their speed ceiling is correspondingly higher.

2 Muscle relaxation. Roughly speaking, two sets of muscles control limb actions. Agonists contract to produce the movement and antagonists relax to allow that movement to occur. If the antagonists don't relax fully, then the action will not reach maximum speed.

3 The ratio of involved muscles to the mass of the limb or body. The muscles of lean persons do not have to move unnecessary weight.

Speed training imposes heavy loads on muscles, tendons and ligaments, so bear these points in mind:

1 Do not begin speed work until you have gone through a thorough and, above all, specific warm-up.

2 Use only light muscle loadings.

3 Do not speed train tired muscles.

You can develop your own speed drills, provided they take note of the following:

1 All movements must be performed at or near maximum/optimum speed, though the highest standard of skill must be maintained. It's no good being really fast if your techniques are rubbish.

2 Speed training achieves the best results when the neuromuscular system is rested. Fatigue reduces the value of speed training.

Therefore, design your drills to allow flat-out work performed over a short enough period to avoid the onset of fatigue. Then allow a long enough active rest period for your energy levels to pump back up again. If you make your work period too long and/or your rest period too short, you will develop varying levels of speed/endurance. This is the ability of your muscles to work quickly in spite of accumulating levels of waste product. Speed/endurance will prove useful during marathon sparring sessions but it may not provide the kind of training effect you need.

Stamina

Any form of physical activity, including speed and strength drills, eventually causes fatigue – especially in the muscles being worked. So you need stamina to cope with the number of repetitions. Achieve improvements here by working muscles over longer and longer periods at different intensities.

Actually, there are two separate yet linked forms of endurance. You can sustain a light training load over long periods because oxygen supply is sufficient to burn muscle fuel efficiently into carbon dioxide and water, and neither of these waste products creates a problem. This kind of endurance is known as 'aerobic' because it depends upon oxygen. Aerobic training is best illustrated by such activities as jogging, cycling or swimming.

Regular aerobic training works the heart muscle, causing it to pump more forcefully, so more blood is circulated to the muscles, supplying more oxygen and washing out carbon dioxide more effectively. Increase the pace of training and eventually oxygen demand outstrips supply. Waste products such as lactic acid then build up more quickly, causing fatigue.

However, the point at which aerobic work effectively tips over into fatigue generating anaerobic activity will depend upon how well developed the aerobic platform is. It therefore makes sound sense to build a good aerobic level of stamina upon which to base high-intensity work.

Increase endurance in targeted muscles by working them hard with heavier weights than those used for speed/strength drills, yet which are light enough for a large number of fast repetitions.

Suppleness

Flexibility training is always the last of the 'S' factors to improve. In practice, training drills aim to increase the range of movement in the hips and spine. Unless any abnormality is present, the shoulders should already be sufficiently flexible for karate purposes.

Just to repeat what I said earlier, supple joints allow a limb to accelerate over a full range of movement (Fig 3), while simultaneously protecting the rapidly stretching muscles from injury. Injury may well result if you reach the limit of your flexibility with no reserve left in hand.

Limitations to the range of movement across a joint arise from the following:

1   The mechanical limits of the joint. These are imposed by the bony structures themselves and they cannot be exceeded without injury.
2   Limitations imposed by the connective tissue that surrounds the joint and holds it together.
3   Tension in the muscle being stretched. In the first instance this arises because the muscle has a safety mechanism that causes it to contract and limit stretching below the point at which the untrained fibre would tear. In the second instance, tension occurs when the muscle tissues are stretched to the limit of their present elasticity.
4   The presence of fatty tissue imposes a physical limit. Loss of this tissue increases the range of movement.

We will be considering how to reduce the limitation imposed by muscle tension, and the first step towards achieving this is to bring the body to a well-exercised and 'warm' state.

Just as there were different types of strength, so there are different kinds of suppleness. The first is static suppleness and we will consider that next.

To achieve static suppleness, we have to work out how best to stretch the relevant muscles. I say 'relevant' because many people blindly perform exercises which will never be able to help them achieve the desired result.

The targeted muscle is then progressively stretched until the point of discomfort is reached. Proceed no further! Any attempt to pass beyond this point will produce a muscular contraction that prevents further stretching.

We can delay the onset of this contraction by gradual movement, rather than by sudden, sharp

Fig 3 **Supple joints allow a full range of movement with less risk of injury.**

actions and even when we reach a final position of maximum stretch, this too can be improved upon through regular training using a neat little drill involving Proprioceptive Neuromuscular Facilitation. This effectively extends the degree to which a muscle can be stretched by reducing the stretch reflex.

Imagine you have reached maximum stretch. Then contract the stretched muscle against the loading. Hold the contraction for 10 seconds, then relax it again and resume the stretch. You will find you have gained anything up to an inch or two of extra stretch by 'fooling' the muscle.

Provided the muscles are thoroughly warmed up and already used to stretching, then PNF exercising will provide dramatic gains in flexibility.

Dynamic suppleness refers to the degree to which your joints will allow movement during technique execution. Unfortunately, what you achieve through static stretching need not necessarily transfer into the kind of dynamic mobility required by skilful karate techniques. That is why you should begin with static training and go on to dynamic drills – but whatever you do, don't reverse this sequence! Think of static stretching as setting limits within which to build dynamic mobility.

Now we've covered the 'S' factors in greater detail, I want to make some general comments about fitness training.

BEFORE SELECTING TRAINING DRILLS

Training is quite specific in its application. Thus, if I run 20 miles a day, I will eventually become a marathon runner. If this also makes me a good karateka, then all well and good – but my guess is that it wouldn't. What I am trying to say is that fitness is a relative term – fitness to punch, to kick high, to train over long periods and to throw a fast block all require highly specific drills performed at regular intervals.

Some drills have unfortunate and hidden side-effects. Thus, you may decide to increase the speed of your punches by wrapping your wrist with light weights. These are quite suitable for speed training, but beware! A fast punch with wrist weights builds up a great deal of momentum energy which must be shed within the criteria of elbow extension/weight distribution. Often this excess energy is dissipated by unwelcome technique modifications.

Therefore, decide what exactly it is you want to do, identify the muscles that need working on, train them in exactly the right way, and look out for any unforeseen side-effects or circumstances. Your best training aides are a knowledge of your body and enough intelligence to use that knowledge effectively.

TRAINING FOR STAMINA

The following drills are suitable for developing stamina in karate, though this is far from being an exhaustive list.

Low-Intensity Stamina Training

The first low-intensity stamina exercise that springs to mind is *kata*. Perform basic *kata* one after the other without a break, adding on at least one advanced *kata* such as *kanku dai*, or its equivalent in your style. Then measure your pulse over a 6-second period. Multiply the number of beats by ten. If your heart rate lies between 130/160 beats a minute, then you are in the aerobic training band. More than this and you are into the fatigue-producing anaerobic band.

You may be very unfit, in which case you simply won't be able to last out. If so, adjust the pace until you can continue for a full 20 minutes. Your heart and lungs will benefit if you do this each day.

If you don't enjoy *kata*, then practise basic techniques instead, alternating kicks with punches to get a spread of muscular involvement. Try shadow boxing or working out on a suspended bag – any technique may be used as long as you raise your pulse into the aerobic band. Using techniques from your martial art to improve stamina you can improve skill at the same time. The general alternatives of running, swimming and cycling do improve aerobic fitness but have few other spin-offs.

High-Intensity Stamina Training

Increasing the pace of training and/or loadings on muscles causes the anaerobic system to take a larger role in energy production, leading to high concentrations of lactic acid in the muscles. So high-intensity stamina drills aim at training your body to reprocess this waste product as quickly as possible while tolerating it in high levels within the working muscles.

Work out harder on the bag, raining barrages of hard punches and kicks on to it. Then take your pulse to check that you are into the anaerobic band. If not, increase your training intensity. The maximum safe pulse rate you can sustain is 220 beats per minute minus your age in years (i.e. 202 beats per minute for an 18 year old).

Keep this up for about 3 minutes, then slow down until your pulse rate drops back into the aerobic band once more. You may find that it drops back quickly (i.e. you are relatively fit), in which case you can resume working flat out after less rest time. Repeat these cycles of work/rest, aiming to cut rest periods back to 1 minute, while increasing the flat-out phases. Classic competition karateka should aim at a flat-out phase of 3 minutes; this being the duration of a bout.

A different version of this drill trains the initial energy supply system which engages whenever you launch into flat-out work from a rested state. Kick a bag with maximum effort for about 15 seconds, then drop back to very light work for a couple of minutes. This gives the body's instant energy supply system time to pump back up again, ready for the next onslaught. Repeat the sequence several times, alternating kicks with punches to get the best training effect.

If you get fed up with using martial art techniques to improve your stamina then select from the many general exercises available. These may prove more efficient at developing stamina but they won't have the spin-off of improving your skill. Here are a few you may like to try.

Drop into a crouch and shoot both legs out behind, adopting a press-up position on the tips of your fingers (Fig 4). Spring forward into a crouch again and jump into the air so both feet leave the ground. Perform at least twenty repetitions, then check your pulse rate to see how the exercise is affecting you. Perform it at less than maximum effort over a longer period for an aerobic effect, or do it quickly and with maximum effort to engage the anaerobic system. This exercise also promotes agility and co-ordination while working the leg muscles explosively.

Drop into a half crouch but don't go any lower or you will unnecessarily stress your knee joints (Fig 5). Then straighten both legs explosively so your feet clear the ground. Jump squats build local endurance and elastic strength into the muscles, stretching them like rubber bands as you sink down, and abruptly contracting them as you shoot back up again. But don't pause in the squat position!

Fig 4 **Take the weight on your fingertips and shoot your legs out behind.**

Fig 5 **Never exceed a half squat.**

Vary the exercise by kicking high as you straighten up, using each leg alternately to deliver the kick.

Any jumping exercise will improve aerobic endurance when repeated for long periods at lower intensities and anaerobic endurance in the leg muscles when performed flat-out for a shorter period.

Local Endurance

As we have seen, squats, or any jumping exercise, can be used to build local endurance in leg muscles. Improve local endurance in the arms and shoulders by practising drills such as sticking hands at the appropriate level of intensity. Alternatively, use exercises such as press-ups. Begin by doing as many press-ups as you can. Speed is not a factor at this stage, so work at a leisurely rate. Give yourself a short active rest, then see how many more press-ups you can do. As you become fitter,

increase loading on your working muscles by placing your feet on a chair (Fig 6). Some martial artists even perform press-ups from a handstand position!

Increase the pace when your chest and upper arm muscles become used to this. Get a partner to time you over, say fifty repetitions, then take an active rest. Repeat the timed session. The working muscles quickly become fatigued, but continuing this drill enables them to continue working in high levels of lactic acid.

One-armed, or explosive press-ups (Fig 7) build elastic strength in the shoulders and upper arms, so alternate series of explosive press-ups with rest periods of normal press-ups.

Vary the training effect of normal press-ups by altering the position of your arms, taking them forward, spreading them wide, or bringing them together (Fig 8)

Use 'the cat' as an active rest exercise between intensive press-up sessions. Skim forward and down between your hands, dropping your thighs to the mat and arching your back (Fig 9). Then push your body backwards and up, so your elbows straighten fully and your backside rises high.

Chins are another excellent shoulder and upper arm exercise but widen the training effect by gripping the bar at different positions and with under/overarm grips

Work your stomach muscles with sit-ups, though always perform them with bent knees. Straight leg sit-ups tilt the pelvis and put a great strain on the lower back. Vary the training effect by bending the knees to differing degrees. Bringing the heels close to the backside loads a different set of muscles more heavily than when the sit-up is made with nearly straight legs.

Follow the same progressive training regime as you would for the press-ups (see above) and when you can manage 100 sit-ups without a break, switch to sit-ups on an inclined surface, or hold a weight to your chest.

STRENGTH TRAINING

The above exercises can also be used as strength training drills, since strength and stamina are

Fig 6   **Increase loading by resting your feet on a chair.**

Fig 7   **Explosive press-ups build elastic strength in the shoulders and upper arms.**

Fig 8   **Vary the training effect of press-ups by bringing your hands together.**

Fig 9   **Lower your hips to the floor and arch your back.**

closely interlinked. It is simply a matter of changing the emphasis. In fact, repeating any exercise that loads a muscle will make it stronger, and the greater the loading, the stronger the muscle becomes. This is important because when you have reached your limit in terms of limb speed, then leaving aside the effects of skill for the moment, further improvements in impact force will only be achieved by increasing the strength of muscle contraction.

We will be looking here at strength training drills of the isotonic type. Specialist isometric drills are used only in cases of joint injury, otherwise they are included into the usage of stances as part of skill training.

Training drills for strength involve either body weight, or external weights. External weights must be light enough to move quickly, otherwise you will develop a slow, powerful contraction rather than a fast one. Also, ensure you are thoroughly warmed up in the correct way before beginning any form of weight training.

Hold the weight bar against the front of your thighs and raise it to your chest by flexing the elbows. Then lower it back and repeat the exercise. Don't cheat by thrusting your thighs forward to bump the bar into an upward motion.

Change your hand position on the bar, holding it near the centre with an over-arm grip. Raise your elbows to draw the weights upwards (Fig 10).

Lie back on a weights bench with the bar across your chest, then quickly thrust it upwards until both elbows lock straight. Always use a spotter to take the weight of the bar from you when you become tired.

Weights make squats into a more demanding exercise so hold the bar behind your neck for one set, and in front for the next. Jump squats with light weights build explosive strength in the leg muscles.

Split squats begin from a forward stance, holding the weight bar across the back of your neck. Jump into the air, changing your feet over in flight so you land in the opposite position. These also build explosive strength in the legs.

Dead lift is a good general weight training exercise. Bend forward and lower the weight bar to the floor, then lift it by straightening up – don't use your elbows.

Half-squat in front of the weight bar and grasp it with both hands. Straighten your legs and lift the bar, then flex your elbows, raising the bar across the front of your chest. Press it above your head, locking both elbows straight. Then lower it to the floor.

The above is only a small selection of training drills using weights to increase strength. By all means import other exercises which will strengthen your muscles in the appropriate way. Work your arm muscles one day, then rest them by switching to leg drills the next, and so on.

SPEED TRAINING

Speed training involves performing technically valid techniques at maximum/optimum speed.

Either have your partner use a target mitt, or face a mirror with the coach holding a buzzer or bell behind his back. Each time he sounds the

Fig 10 **Hold the bar near the centre and draw your elbows up.**

buzzer, execute a full-speed but good quality technique, using the mirror or your partner to check your form. The coach should allow a brief rest before pressing the buzzer again. The length of this rest must be varied to prevent you from jumping the gun, though it should never be so short that you cannot recock the technique.

Switch sides when there is an obvious fall-off in the speed of your techniques, or take an active rest period.

Use ankle or wrist weights carefully, because unless they are very light, they may cause you to make unwelcome technique modifications. The same comments apply to drills using elastic straps or draw ropes. Heavier weights reduce the speed of technique execution and so are useless in this context.

Train for whole body fast movement by sprinting on the spot for 10/15 seconds, while pumping elbows and knees as high as possible. Allow a full active rest before repeating the sprint. Alternatively, use your belt to tow your training partner behind you as you spring forward from stance to stance. If no partner is available, try sprinting up a steep hill or wading quickly through water.

Reaction Time

Speed training must include reaction time drills since the fastest technique in the world is of little value if it is delivered long after the opponent has moved position! The skilled karateka sees and identifies the opponent's movement at the earliest possible time, and selects a suitable technique to deal with it. In practical terms, the more experience you have at sparring, the more your body will learn to react automatically. This, of course, presupposes that you already have the necessary skill to perform techniques properly.

Use a partner to train for reaction speed. Your partner holds a pair of target mitts face down on his thighs and, without any warning, swings either one of them up so it is briefly presented face or edge on at varying heights. Hit it quickly, accurately and with control, using either a kick or strike/punch (Fig 11).

The second training drill has the partner holding an impact pad against his chest as he moves forward or back with short, sharp movements.

Fig 11 **Hit the target mitt quickly and with the appropriate technique.**

Maintain your distance and range your punch accurately on the pad.

FLEXIBILITY TRAINING

Static Training Drills

Static training aims at creating a platform of basic suppleness upon which you can develop more relevant flexibility, and you can either work alone, or with a trusted partner. In both cases, the limit of flexibility must be reached slowly and held for at least 10 seconds. Try for longer if you can manage it, because the longer you hold maximum stretch, the greater the training effect. Finally, do not attempt to proceed through the pain barrier. This will cause you damage and slow your flexibility programme down.

Many of the exercises described in this section stretch different muscle groups in different ways. Thus, an exercise aimed at stretching the hamstrings will also stretch the muscles of the spine. And so on.

The following exercises may be performed without a partner.

Step forward into a long, low forward stance. Turn your hips to the front, but do not allow the rear heel to lift. Lower your hips as much as possible (Fig 12).

Turn your hips to the front and lower your weight over the supporting leg, allowing the other to straighten out (Fig 13). Then move your weight to the other leg.

This performs several stretches simultaneously. It is particularly good for ankle flexibility in that the sole of your supporting foot is kept flat on the floor as you sink down. It also opens the hip of the supporting leg, while stretching the hamstring of the extended leg. When time is short and you must be selective, choose this exercise above all others.

Sit down and stretch both legs out fully. Bring them together and press them down to the floor. Take both arms forward and together, so they lie directly above the legs. Then 'dive' forward, trying to extend your fingertips as far beyond your toes as possible. Really push those arms forward and hold maximum stretch for as long as possible. Don't jerk forward since this stimulates the muscles' safety mechanism, causing them to shorten and tighten.

Remain in the sitting position, but open your legs as wide as possible. Dive forward between your legs with reaching hands and when you are at full stretch, sweep your hands from side to side, so they touch each ankle.

Bring both legs back together again and draw one back, so it lies at 90° to the extended leg. Tuck the heel of the withdrawn foot against your backside. Now lower your head on to the leading knee and hold it there for a slow count of ten. Straighten your back, then lower your head on to the flexed knee of the other leg. Hold the lowest position for ten, then straighten once more. Finally, lower your head between both knees and hold for a final count of ten (Fig 14). Repeat the exercise several times, then change leading legs and begin again.

Here is a truly excellent exercise for improving hip flexibility.

Lay on your back, so your backside is close to a wall. Extend your legs up the wall, then let gravity open them out. Look at any object over your

Fig 12 **Lower your hips in order to stretch the thigh muscles**

Fig 13 **Lean forward between your legs to keep balance.**

shoulder and try to relax the leg muscles as much as possible (Fig 15). When they begin to ache, lift both legs slightly against the force of gravity, holding them until the muscles begin to quiver with the strain. Then relax and allow gravity to take over once more. You will discover that your legs now open wider than they did the first time. However, do be aware that the muscles are now prone to injury and must not be overworked.

A final word of warning about the last exercise. Because the force of gravity works insidiously, it is easily possible to over stretch the muscles, producing some interesting bruises.

Support yourself on hands and knees. Then open your knees as wide as possible, and gently move your hips back and forth between them. This has a similar effect to the previous exercise, though it is neither so fierce nor so punishing to knee joints.

Static Training Drills Using A Partner

We will now look at some exercises which use a partner. In all cases, the partner applies smooth and steady pressure to the point where discomfort sets in, at which point he stops!

Begin with your back against the wall and offer your extended leg to your partner. He takes your heel on his shoulder and holds your knee straight. Then he gradually straightens his back and lifts your leg as high as possible. Aim to touch the wall above your head with the ball of your foot, holding it there for a count of ten.

This exercise loses its training effect the instant your supporting heel lifts. Repeat the exercise five times on both legs.

Vary the training effect by standing sideways to the wall and offering your foot in side-kick configuration. As before, your partner lifts it steadily to maximum height and holds it there for a count of ten (Fig 16).

There are many variations of this exercise, one of which sits pairs of partners facing each other

Fig 14 **Lower head between both knees and hold it there for a minimum 10-count.**

Fig 15 **Relax and let the gradual effect of gravity fully open your legs.**

Fig 16 **Your partner gradually lifts the extended leg.**

with legs outstretched and soles of feet together. Pull on your partner's arms and shoulders, and try to bring your hips closer together. Shorter people can put their feet slightly inside the taller partner's.

Sit down and tuck your feet close in to your backside with the soles together. Then reach forward and take hold of your feet. Your partner stands behind or in front of you and places his hands on your knees; then he presses smoothly downwards. Allow your knees to open out to maximum, holding this position for a count of ten. Then resist the downward push, forcing your knees strongly upwards for a second count of ten before relaxing once more.

This exercise is making use of the PNF effect.

There are are many other flexibility exercises which you may come across.

Dynamic Mobility Training

I now want to discuss dynamic mobility exercises. Think of these as flexibility exercises in action, as

it were. Straight leg swings, whether to the front, side or back are typical general exercises but note that they are not intended to increase flexibility; rather, they ensure a smooth movement within the limits of flexibility achieved by static stretching. Perform very high front kicks, side kicks and roundhouse kicks with a light snapping action rather than a thrust. Technique form should be exact, despite the intentional lack of power.

Twist the spine from side to side, extending your arms and turning so they point behind you. Move smoothly between the limits of flexibility. Link your hands back to back and thrust them upwards as far as possible. Lean first to one side, then to the other (Fig 17). Keep your hands extended and move your trunk in a circle which travels first in one direction before reversing and going the other way. Vary this exercise by letting your hands separate and trailing them as you circle your trunk.

Fig 17 **Interlink your fingers and lean first to one side, then to the other.**

That concludes discussion of training drills to improve the 'S' factors. I now want to talk about another aspect of fitness important to karateka.

AGILITY TRAINING

For our purposes here, agility training refers to the ability of a skilled karateka to employ a wide range of effective techniques in whatever order and form suits the circumstances. This requires the ability to change stances while performing skilled and complex movements with the limbs.

Karate techniques are an excellent source of agility training. Thus, if you normally perform a sequence in the order front kick/snap punch, then agility train by learning how to perform the sequence equally well backwards! Similarly, if you normally practise front kick/roundhouse kick/reverse punch, try reversing the order.

In other words, break up the normal technique sequences to which you have become accustomed and learn to perform them effectively, in any order and in any direction.

Some people perform kata backwards. Others switch, on command from the coach, from kata to kata. These are all excellent ways of improving your agility.

WARM-UP AND COOL-DOWN

You should never begin any kind of training without first warming up. The purpose of this is to gradually accustom the tissues to the level of work that will be required of them during training proper. Warm-up is not intended to take too much out of you, so set a gradually increasing pace, culminating at a comfortable level. Begin with gentle movements – not those which involve explosive action, and choose exercises which are appropriate to the techniques and drills you will be working on. Choose a sensible length for warm-up, say 10 minutes per 90 minutes of practice.

Allow a similar period in which to cool-down after training. A thorough cool-down allows increased blood flow to flush out waste materials from working muscles instead of leaving them locked away to cause stiffness the next day. Gentle stretching exercises are ideal for the final stages of cool-down, finishing off finally with meditation.

Cool-down also returns the karateka to a fit mental state in which to re-enter the outside world!

A good training plan is therefore meditation, warm-up, speed, strength and stamina drills, first half of karate training proper, suppleness and dynamic mobility drills, second half of karate training proper, cool-down, meditation and finish. But bear in mind that the sensible karateka will use karate techniques in his 'S' factor training drills, so he acquires skill at the same time.

And that's where we started this chapter!

4

WORKING WITH STANCES

INTRODUCTION

Both classical and freestyle karate lay great emphasis on stances – that is, the way the feet and hands are arranged so as to produce a posture and guard suitable for the execution of particular techniques. Unfortunately, however, classical karate seems to emphasise the importance of stance for its own sake. What I mean by this is that classical stances are most closely scrutinised when the person is standing motionless – an artificial situation not found in actual practice.

In freestyle karate, stances are seen as platforms for technique execution – not as ends in themselves. And just as techniques are never frozen during their performance, so stances are neither fixed nor static.

A useful analogy to see how the correct use of stance relates to effective technique is a comparison with the valves in the cylinder head of a car engine. When the engine is running, these are on the valve seat for only tiny fractions of a second, yet even a tiny imperfection in a single valve face reduces compression and measurably damages power output.

A good stance will allow you to strike forcefully from whichever position you are in, because through it, the whole body is able to support critical arm and leg actions. Without this support, techniques will be weak, or at best, possess only local energy.

Correct use of stance means many different things as follows:

1   Control over your centre of gravity.
2   Allowing attacks to be evaded.
3   Opening or closing engagement distances.
4   Adopting the correct line.
5   Being able to use a wide range of techniques.

But correct use of stance means more than just taking up a particular posture, it also involves movement. A punch or kick delivered with your centre of gravity moving behind it will be more powerful, while the correct weight distribution means a faster technique and fewer tell-tale cues to warn the opponent.

Classical karate's overriding emphasis on stability probably comes from its roots in southern Shaolin kung fu, where the emphasis is on strong hand techniques performed from a firm platform. A low centre of gravity does indeed provide stability, but on the other side of the coin, it both makes for relatively slow movements and inhibits fast kicking. And since fast kicks are a part of karate's armoury, then it follows that low stances must be unsuitable.

Do not forget that karate is a hybrid system. It incorporated high kicks from other sources at a later stage in its development, and then tried to make them work from its hand technique oriented stances.

Some stances are used because of their imagined training effect. First example: low stances are said to strengthen the upper leg muscles and since these help locate the knee, then it follows that low stances must be good for the knee. My response is that while the knee does need all the help it can get to cope with classical karate practice, there are far better ways of strengthening it. Second example: practising *sanchin* will develop an immovable stance. My response to that is, who needs an immovable stance?

This leads us to the next point which is that of the often faulty reasoning behind classical stance work. It used to be said that a long stance was better able to soak up the recoil of a powerful punch, yet leading karateka such as Tommy Morris are able to convincingly show that a rigid stance is not as important as one in which the centre of gravity is moving behind the technique. Indeed, it is possible to strike with considerable force when only one foot is in contact with the ground – and this flies very much in the face of classical thinking on the matter.

Try the following experiment: take up a long left forward stance of the type favoured by Shotokan and lock out your left arm on full extension. Close your fingers into a fist and have your partner advance on it until the fist presses against his chest. Then have him push hard against your fist while you resist. If he applies enough force, you will not be able to prevent your front foot from lifting. But if your leading knee overlies your toes, then your front foot will not rise – no matter how hard your partner pushes.

This example is used by an innovative style of classical karate to show how basic thinking about resistance to recoil is wrong. But I'm not sure that it succeeds because one can never be certain how far you can extrapolate results from a static experiment like this to the dynamics of an actual punching action. But one thing it does do is to show how the Shotokan claim is wrong even on its own reasoning. It shows that it is not so much the length of stance that is important; the position of the centre of gravity is actually the crucial point.

A further problem of classical practice is the way in which it tends to link certain techniques to certain stances. It is a fact that certain stances predispose the use of certain techniques, but even so, we must, from an early stage, learn how to perform techniques from a wide variety of compatible stances.

Yet another problem with classical stance work hinges upon its insistence that a particular stance template must be accurately reproduced. Clearly, this does not take into account the fact that people are all built differently. More important for our purposes is to work out what the stance is supposed to do and then customise it to suit our build. It's surely less important to argue over such things as whether the foot should lie flat on the floor, or whether the heel is raised.

I know some classical karateka will dispute this, and claim that there are good reasons for these details. Some argue that formal stances are part of the building up of correct technique – that we should learn the mechanics of lunge punch from a forward stance because it will prepare us to perform more practical techniques later on. This, of course, is simply not so. For one technique to act as a springboard for another, the two must be sufficiently similar so that the skills involved in learning one are transferred to the other. However, lunge punch from a forward stance is quite unlike the powerful jabs we might use in a realistic sparring situation, so there is little, if any, transference of skill between the two.

CHARACTERISTICS OF THE EFFECTIVE STANCE

Though karate competition is itself highly artificial, nevertheless it more closely approaches reality than does basic technique. And if we look at competition, we see that classical stances are little in evidence. Instead, we will tend to see medium to high stances because these allow us to adjust range and line etc. quickly. They have enough lateral component (side-step) to give a small amount of side-to-side stability, though not at the expense of exposing the groin to attack.

I don't know how much more we can safely extrapolate from classic competition karate since it prohibits groin and face attacks, and this safeguard is reflected in the stances and guards now employed. Presumably in a realistic sparring situation, both face and groin would become prime targets, and so would have to be adequately protected by means of a different stance and guard.

Even so I think we can say that an effective stance must present a narrow target profile to the opponent, so this rules out standing square-on to him. At the other extreme, though a sideways-facing stance provides a small target profile, it withdraws two body weapons from immediate use, while turning the body's centre line away from the opponent. A compromise between these two extremes is therefore the one to go for and I would suggest that the most effective is probably closer to square-on than sideways-on.

Centre Line

This is a good place to talk about the importance of centre line. Curiously, this key concept of southern Shaolin kung fu is missing from the karate it gave rise to, so it is very much up to freestyle karate to reintroduce it.

Imagine an opponent standing in front of you, with his arms hanging at his sides. Draw an imaginary vertical line down through his head and body, separating him into two equal halves. This line is his centre line and while it faces you, the opponent can use all his body weapons to the maximum effect. But bear in mind the disadvantages of standing square-on.

The human body is built for moving forwards, not sideways like a crab, so it will tend to develop its maximum power in a forward direction. There-fore, the further the opponent's centre line is turned from you, the weaker becomes his offensive and defensive capability. By all means try this out and see for yourself whether a forwards-facing stance gives you greater versatility and whole body power than a sideways-facing stance.

Height And Weight Distribution

Should the stance be high or low? We have already seen how a low stance is well suited to the more massive person who likes to stand his ground and use hand techniques. But what if you have a low body mass, good agility and mobile hips? If this sounds more like you, then consider adopting a high stance. A high stance has a high centre of gravity and so is inherently unstable. This is a disadvantage for the heavy puncher, but an advantage for the light kicker. If you are between these two extremes, then choose the one that suits you best.

But regardless of the height you finally settle on, weight distribution will remain around fifty/fifty between leading and trailing leg. Only with this can you achieve maximum versatility. Your centre of gravity may move forwards when you throw a punch, or backwards when you withdraw from a technique, but always it will quickly return to the mid-way position.

Harnessing Elastic Strength To Stances

Only a supremely confident person can safely stand motionless as the opponent selects a better line and fighting distance. The rest of us will be constantly readjusting our distance and line to cope with the opponent's movements. The trick is always to move lightly and on the balls of your feet, with knees flexed to stretch the muscles on the front of your thighs. This preloads them with latent power, so they are ready to explode in the chosen direction.

Some people overdo this, and jump up and down with a regular rhythm. This is not safe because the astute opponent will anticipate your next upwards movement and rush in at that point.

TYPES OF STANCE

I now want to look at the various stances used in both classical and freestyle karate.

In general terms, there are two types of stance: the ritual and the practical. Ritual stances are used to express courtesy to the teacher; courtesy in the form of polite attention while he is speaking, and courtesy in the form of a greetings ritual that begins and ends training. Since the latter is Eastern in origin, some Western students will find it odd and the freestyle coach may decide to replace it with more familiar ways of beginning training.

A typical attention stance is erect, with the heels of the feet together and the palms of the hands pressed flat against the front of the thighs. The back is straight, the shoulders are relaxed and the head is lifted (Fig 18). This stance is adopted whenever the coach is giving directions, or is about to give directions. It shows alertness and a proper sense of self.

Some karate schools use a standing bow to signal respect. If yours is one of these, then simply incline your upper body forwards while keeping your eyes fixed on the object of your respect. Pause at the lowest point, then return smoothly to an upright position once more. Do not hurry the standing bow, or make it jerky.

If your school precedes and/or follows training sessions with periods of kneeling meditation, then follow the steps outlined below.

Take up the kneeling position by opening your knees as you squat down. Then press the right knee to the floor, followed by the left. Lower your body on to the backs of the calves with your feet pointing straight out behind (Fig 19). It is not a good idea to flex your ankles so the balls of the feet press to the floor. This eases pressure on the

ankles – but beware in case someone steps on your Achilles' tendons. This may injure flexed ankles but not extended feet.

It is most important that you keep your back upright. Relax your shoulders but don't slouch. Lift your head and look towards the instructor. Press the palms of your hands against the front of your thighs.

If you find kneeling stance difficult to maintain for the whole period of meditation, then practise at home, initially using a cushion to give your ankles support.

Classical karate requires the class to perform a series of bows from kneeling position. Typically, the first is to the founder of the style, the second is to the instructor and the third is to the other students with whom you will be practising. I have included a description of the ritual for those students who train at clubs where it is followed.

On the command, incline your upper body slowly forward, sliding your hands forward and resting them palm-downwards on the floor. The fingertips of both hands are close together. Keep your eyes on the instructor at all times in recognition of the fact that the warrior was taught never

Fig 19   **Kneel with your back upright and your feet extended.**

to relax his vigilance. Pause at the lowest point of the bow and then return smoothly to the upright-kneeling position you started from. Wait for further directions, then get to your feet in the reverse sequence that you used to kneel. Take up a formal attention stance once more.

Typically, training will now begin and so you move to the next stage of readiness. Slide your left, then your right foot to the side until they are shoulder width apart. Weight is evenly distributed over both feet. Roll your hands into loose fists (Fig 20).

You can use this formal ready stance when you feel you might be attacked, yet do not wish to make your state of readiness obvious. Stand 25° or so from directly facing a potential opponent to ensure both a narrower target profile and that your centre line is not turned too far away from him. Clasp your hands together in front of your groin.

Ready stance is therefore a bridge between ritual stances and more practical postures.

Improve fore and aft stability by taking a half-step forward with either foot into walking stance. Bodyweight shifts forward with the advancing foot and comes to rest midway between them (Fig 21). Note that this stance has both length (the half

step forward) and width. The latter derives from the width of ready stance from which you started.

Walking stance has more stability than ready stance, so it can resist pushes from the front and back, as well as from either side. The knees are not flexed though, so there is little explosive potential in the upper leg muscles. The body faces almost square-on to the opponent, so all your body weapons can be quickly deployed. Having said that, it also presents the opponent with a fairly large target profile.

Slide your leading foot a further half step forward but maintain the same width. Twist both feet until they are parallel but turned to a slight angle from dead ahead. Use a mirror to check you are getting the best compromise between groin coverage/target profile, while keeping your centre line turned towards the opponent. Flex your knees equally so the stance is lower and has potential energy (Fig 22).

What we have now is an unspecialised fighting stance that is well suited to fast movement in all directions. Because it is longer than walking stance, it provides better stability in the face of the opponent's advance, and because it has a width component, your balance is not precarious. Fighting stance is *the* basic stance of freestyle karate. It

Fig 20 **Move your feet a shoulder width apart and clench your fists. This is 'ready stance'.**

Fig 21 **Step forward a half pace into 'walking stance'.**

Fig 22 **Fighting stance has both knees bent and ready for explosive movement.**

Fig 23 **Forward stance is too rigid for the cut and thrust of free sparring.**

Fig 24 **Back stance turns your hips away from the opponent.**

Fig 25 **Make back stance safer by turning your hips square-on.**

is used as a platform for practising the basic techniques in the same way that the more rigid forward stance is used in the classical schools.

Now take up a forward stance by further advancing your leading foot until it is a good pace and a half in front of the trailing one. Turn your hips square-on, using the rear leg as a prop. The extent to which the trailing knee joint straightens will, of course, vary according to the length of the stance. In longer forward stances, the rear knee is absolutely straight, while in shorter versions it may bend slightly. Move your centre of gravity forwards and bend the front knee until it overlies the toes. Provided you have turned your hips to face square-on, then the rear foot will face diagonally forwards while the front foot points directly ahead. Relax your shoulders.

Forward stance (Fig 23) is transient in freestyle karate. That is to say it is held only for instants of time. Because it is long, it is also rigid and slow to move from. Use it if you want to reach for the opponent with a hand technique. Use it also if you want to stand your ground as the opponent rushes into you.

Forward stance is quite powerful because your centre line is turned forwards and all your hand weapons are available for immediate use – but don't remain in it for too long. Now draw your centre of gravity back towards the rear leg, pulling the front foot back and slightly inwards until all side-step vanishes. Both knees are now bent, but the rear is flexed more than the front. The rear leg supports 60 per cent of body weight and the front leg the remainder. Typically the hips rotate so the centre line turns away from the opponent (Fig 24).

'Back stance' is normally used in classical karate when you want to withdraw your face and body just slightly from the opponent – though I would not advise ever using it! Since it has no width component, it is unstable with regard to side-to-side forces, but worse, with the centre line turned so far from the opponent, the stance is very weak and two body weapons are made unavailable for immediate use. Improve it by turning your hips back towards the opponent (Fig 25). This shortens the stance and brings more weight over the rear leg.

Continue withdrawing your leading foot until 90 per cent body weight rests over the rear foot. Bend the supporting knee yet further, so the stance is quite low. Keep your back straight and don't let your backside stick out. Turn your hips

Fig 26 **Draw back your leading foot and raise the heel from the floor.**

Fig 27 **Momentarily lift one foot clear of the floor.**

Fig 28 **Keep your back straight and force your knees outwards.**

fully forward-facing and lift the heel of the leading foot from the floor (Fig 26).

'Cat stance' is taken up only for instants of time because, although your centre line now faces the opponent, you are not in a good state of balance. Use it to draw back from the opponent's kick or punch, then move immediately into him with a counter attack. Use cat stance also to deliver fast front foot kicks, but with the sole exception of groin kick, whether such techniques are ever truly effective is difficult to say. Even so, always use cat stance in preference to back stance because of its better presentation of centre line.

The ultimate in transient stances must surely be 'crane stance', in which all the weight is transferred to the bent back leg and the front foot is lifted clear of the floor (Fig 27). Use this when the opponent attempts to sweep your front foot, lifting it over his and then dropping it forwards as you perform a strong counter-attack.

Withdraw your leading foot all the way back to ready stance which, as you will recall, has the feet shoulder width apart. Then step out alternately with the left and right feet until the stance is much wider. Now bend your knees and sink down, keeping your back upright and your backside tucked in. Your feet are splayed outwards, paralleling the line of your thighs. Push your knees outwards – do not let them collapse inwards. Try to make sure your knees are directly above your ankles (Fig 28).

Straddle stance presents a narrow target profile to the opponent, but that is the only point in its favour. Your centre line is now a full 90° from the opponent and two of your body weapons are not immediately available. In fact, the only reason I described this stance is because you may inadvertently find yourself in it after a turning kick has missed. And secondly, the opponent may begin his attack from the side, meaning that you may need to be able to do something, at least, from that position.

MOVING BETWEEN STANCES

All movements between stances involve moving one or both feet. Therefore, move them quickly and, wherever possible, mask the movement with a feint. Your feet should always just skim the floor – they never lift from it. In the following descriptions, all movements begin from fighting stance.

Short Movements Between Stances

Switch-changing the stance is quite effective for confusing the opponent. To do this, just take a little jump to free the feet, switch them over and land in the opposite stance. Disguise the opening move with a short jab off the front fist and launch your attack proper as your knees flex – because that is when your muscles are most pumped up. However, don't jump higher than necessary and don't set up a predictable rhythm.

Whereas switch-changing the stance involves very little actual movement, you can make small but definite advances and withdrawals by 'arrow walking'. This involves sliding the front foot forward a half step, then drawing the rear up after it. Both parts of the step must be equal in length or successive stances will gradually get longer or shorter. Use this method to close range before engagement begins – but be careful not to set up an obvious rhythm that cues the opponent!

The front foot slide uses a thrusting action of the bent trailing knee, resisted by the friction of the leading foot against the floor. Reduce that friction by lifting the front foot slightly so the trailing leg thrusts you a short distance into forward stance. But don't lift your foot too high – just let it skim over the floor. You don't need to gather up the rear foot immediately; use it as a prop for a long-ranging jab to the opponent's face. Don't lean forward and offer your chin as an inviting target!

A reverse slide uses pressure generated by the leading knee to drive you back a short distance from the opponent's attack. Draw your leading foot back quickly to re-establish a fighting stance.

The front foot angled slide is a little more sophisticated and trades on the notion of line which we will discuss shortly. Begin from a fighting stance and thrust your leading foot forward as above. But this time, angle your sliding foot so the toes point inwards (Fig 29). Then twist your hips and shoulders behind a front hand punch, so your trailing foot slides across. Your finished position is exactly the same as before, except that you have moved out of the opponent's line while turning your own centre line towards him.

Diagonal slides take you to the side of the opponent's attack, yet leave you close enough to make your own response quickly. The object is always to avoid the opponent's attack by the minimum necessary distance – a miss is as good as a mile!

A forward diagonal slide is very similar to the front foot angled slide described above, except that you thrust your leading foot forwards and

Fig 29 **Slide your leading foot forward and turn the toes inwards.**

Fig 30 **Slide your leading foot diagonally forwards and outwards.**

Fig 31 **Slide your trailing foot diagonally backwards and outwards.**

outwards (Fig 30). Turn your foot as before and twist your centre line back towards the opponent. Forward diagonal slide gives a wider margin of safety than the front foot angled slide.

Practise a diagonal slide to the rear by stepping diagonally backwards/outwards with the trailing foot (Fig 31), then withdraw the leading foot to reconstitute fighting stance. Note that your centre line never deviates from facing the opponent.

Side-steps, as their name implies, take you to either side of the opponent's advance. Use these when the opponent throws a kick, or is otherwise strongly moving forward. In such cases, a diagonal slide may be inappropriate because it actually takes you past the opponent. Therefore, step to the left side with your leading left foot (Fig 32) and twist your centre line towards the opponent (Fig 33) Allow your trailing leg to slide right around until your original stance is reconstituted, and use a mirror to check this is so.

Alternatively, step to the right with your trailing right foot, then twist your hips and draw the left back into line.

A final way of covering a short distance uses a slide on the supporting leg, but since this is intimately bound up with technique performance, I have left it until chapter 7 when I look at kicks.

Long Movements Between Stances

You can, of course, simply use an actual step forwards into the opponent, or a step back from him. In either case, disguise your movement with a jab off the leading guard hand. Keep your knees bent as you move and change your guard as you step into the opposite stance. Remember: the higher your fighting stance, the faster you can move!

The length of your step forward or back (as with the length of the slides looked at above) is related to the distance you want to cover. Take a long step if you are attempting to run down the opponent, but draw up your trailing leg to prevent the stance stretching out and becoming unwieldy.

Diagonal steps forward and to the rear have the same beneficial effects as the slides. Simply step diagonally but angle your advancing foot towards the opponent as it sets down. Then throw your hips and shoulders into a punch or block, so your centre line twists to point directly towards him.

Skip-changing the stance is a very fast way of covering a full step forward. It is also useful should you wish to pull back equally quickly. Begin from fighting stance with a short, skimming jump with the right trailing foot. At the same time,

Fig 32 **Step to the side with your left foot.**

Fig 33 **Centre line twist and punch.**

Fig 34 **Jump forwards with your right foot and lift your left knee.**

Fig 35 **Bring your trailing foot forward and turn it outwards.**

Fig 36 **Slide your trailing foot behind the supporting foot to turn the hips away.**

lift your left knee into a kicking position (Fig 34). Disguise the jump forwards with a jab into the opponent's face and time things so the kick impacts just as you land. Use recoil to return to the original stance.

The idea behind timing things this way is to make use of the energy of your moving body to add power to the kick. You recall that in Chapter 3 I talked about how to make your body mass effectively greater by moving your centre of gravity. This is a way of doing just that!

The final method of moving between stances I want to consider is the 'scissors step' – Take up a left fighting stance, then bring your right foot forwards until it comes to lie alongside – or passes – your left foot (Fig 35). Vary the length of the step to suit the distance to be covered. Turn your right foot outwards by 45° and keep both knees bent, so you don't bob up and down. Don't allow your elbows to move away from your sides and keep your shoulders relaxed throughout. Use this version of the scissors step to deliver a front kick to an opponent who might otherwise be out of range.

Gradually increase the speed of the scissors step until your right foot executes a low skimming hop that both covers distance quickly and generates

considerable kinetic energy. Used in this way, the step forward is an accelerator of body mass, but to benefit, the kick must land as full weight is settling on to the other foot.

Use scissors step also from a straddle stance, but this time bring the trailing leg behind the leading foot (Fig 36). This has the effect of turning your hips (and centre line!) away from the opponent, and though a dangerous position to be in, it nevertheless provides a good set-up for side-thrusting kick. Stepping across the front of the leading foot would not engage the hips to the same extent and it is difficult to know what technique you might then use as an effective follow-up.

TURNING FROM STANCE TO STANCE

Turns may be made in a number of ways. The most common is to look over your shoulder to where you are turning, and then simply step across with the rear foot, sliding it an equal distance from one side of the leading leg to the other (Fig 37). Note that the sliding foot rests lightly on the ball of the foot, with the heel lifted well clear of the floor.

45

Fig 37 **Look over your shoulder and slide your trailing foot across.**

Flex both knees and begin the turning motion from the hips. The shoulders lag behind momentarily, making use of torsional stress in the spine to generate additional power, then they swing around and a new guard is taken up. Make turns greater than 180° by sliding the rear foot still further across.

Use front foot turns to give a fast, 90° change of direction. Simply slide your leading foot to the new position, then follow with your hips and shoulders. Maintain an effective guard throughout.

GUARD

'Guard' refers to the disposition of the hands in relation to the stance. One guard hand generally leads the other to provide an early response to the opponent. It can do this because it is further out from your body and is thereby correspondingly closer to the opponent. But don't advance it to the point where the elbow is straight because first,

you will have no reserve of elbow action from which to make a fast jabbing punch and secondly, the opponent can grab your wrist and pull you off balance.

The leading hand is held at chin height and always on its own side of the projected centre line of the body. Crossing the centre line leads inevitably to a weaker guard – so turn your body to close off any vulnerable areas rather than allowing your guard hands to cross.

As its name implies, the rear guard hand is held closer to the body on its own side of the centre line, to provide a second barrier to incoming attacks. Carry your fist close to the side of your jaw and flex the elbow so you can deliver an immediate and powerful punch.

Remember always to lead with the same fist as the forward foot; so if your left foot leads, then your left fist leads too. Any deviation from this gives poor defensive coverage. Keep this in mind and always adjust your guard as you change your stance (see Fig 22 again)

Always maintain some sort of a guard, no matter which stance you are in.

The novice has little control over his arms so they move from side to side and cross the centre line repeatedly. This makes it difficult to respond effectively to the opponent. Economy of movement is very important and is best seen on those occasions when you miss the opponent with a punch – your fist does not shoot on past his ear! Similarly, withdraw your spent technique only so far as is necessary to 'cock' it once more. Remember – whether going back, forward, to the left, to the right or on the diagonals, all your movements must be in proportion. Only when this happens can you regard yourself as competent.

THE CLOSED AND OPEN SIDES OF STANCE

A stance is said to have both a 'closed' and an 'open' side. Visualise the opponent facing you in left fighting stance (see again Fig 22) with his left foot/left guard hand leading. Few easy targets are available on his left side because his left elbow is close to his body, making roundhouse kicks into the ribs awkward. There is only the smallest of

Fig 38   **Always move to the opponent's closed side where he can reach you only with difficulty.**

Fig 39   **Moving to his open side brings you into range of his body weapons.**

targets for a front kick and you are almost certain to strike his elbow with your toes in the attempt! Kicks to the head must first clear both his left elbow and his shoulder. For this reason, the left side of his body is said to be 'closed'.

Though scarcely better, his right side nevertheless presents more opportunities, with a large area of the right rib-cage exposed to a roundhouse kick. And if you can get him to drop his rear guard slightly, a head kick begins to look like a distinct possibility. For this reason, his right is said to be the 'open side'.

Always try to move to the opponent's closed side, since he will then have to twist around to use any of his body weapons effectively (Fig 38). Moving to his open side, however, brings you into range of his right fist and leg (Fig 39). Learn to make this crucial distinction!

LINE

'Line' refers to the positions taken up by two fighters with respect to one another. Begin from left fighting stance and in the first scenario, my leading foot is in line with your trailing foot (and vice versa). In other words, we are directly facing each other (Fig 40). From this position, we both have an equal opportunity to use all our body weapons and neither has an advantage over the other.

In the second scenario, I step slightly to the right with both feet, so my leading foot is now in line with yours. Then I turn slightly so I face you directly once more (Fig 41). Now I can use all my body weapons effectively but you must first turn slightly to reach me. So, by this means I have gained a significant advantage.

Fig 40   From this position, both fighters have an equal opportunity to use their techniques.

Fig 41 **By stepping to the outside of your leading foot, the opponent gains a definite advantage.**

Three points are relevant here. The first is that if I make my side-step obvious, you will notice it and turn your body by the corresponding amount. Therefore, combine changes in line with disguising movements of the hands, or such like. The second point is that I cannot expect you to remain stationary the whole time, so setting up my line is not simply a one-time exercise – I must constantly update it. The third point is that my line always makes use of the distinction between your closed and open sides.

The key issue in using line is try and keep the centre line of my body turned towards you, while ensuring that your centre line is turned away from me. Again, I cannot stress the importance of the centre line enough because it is a crucial part of

maintaining a strong position. If you turn your centre line away under the opponent's attack, then you will be unable to use full body power to counter him. Instead, you will be forced to rely upon the power you can generate in individual limbs – and this may not be enough.

TIMING AND DISTANCE

The object behind timing is to know the best time to attack the opponent.

If the opponent throws a powerful kick at you, you will be able to note some three phases in its performance. The first is the acceleration phase, when his knee is rising to the correct height. The second phase is the kick proper, when his foot travels towards you, and the third is when he tries to recover the spent kick. The first and last phases are both prime windows of opportunity for a counter-attack, and correct timing will allow you to maximise that opportunity.

Provided you are at the correct distance from the opponent, then you should be able to move even as he begins his technique, sliding forward and stop punching his kick before the knee has had chance to rise to its delivery height (Fig 42). He will be committing all his energies to an effective kick and so will be taken unawares by your slide forward.

Again, provided you have not moved too far away, you can close with the opponent immediately his kick has missed you. Kicks take a finite time to recover, during which you can effect a counter. But once the opponent sets his foot down, then his defensive screen becomes fully operational once more.

You can, of course, choose to counter the technique while it is in full flight, using one of the methods of stepping described above. If you do, then beware of blocking the technique directly – body evasion alone should be sufficient. Many arm and hand injuries have resulted from attempts to deflect a powerful kick. Of course, you can deflect them – but why take an unnecessary risk? Deflect a powerful kick only when there is no other option.

It is no use moving at the correct time if you are so far away that it takes ages to close into effective

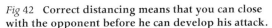

Fig 42 **Correct distancing means that you can close with the opponent before he can develop his attack.**

Fig 43 **It is sufficient for the technique to miss by the minimum distance.**

range. So always evade by the minimum effective distance. Remember that a technique is aimed more or less accurately at a target and moving that target even by the smallest amount is often enough to make the technique miss. But having said that, you must move those few centimetres in the correct direction! Side-step may cause a straight punch or kick to miss, but it could also take you directly into the path of a circling kick or punch.

Learning to move by the minimum amount in the correct direction is a skill that comes only after a great amount of practice, and now is the time to put into effect all the various stances and movements that we have studied.

Take it in turns with your partner to attack and defend, but make sure you both know whose turn it is to do which. The attacker moves smoothly forward from a variety of stances and attempts to push you in the chest with the palm of either

hand. Respond with a combination of stance, timing, distance and movement to cause that push to miss by the minimum effective distance (Fig 43). Touch the opponent lightly as he misses.

Begin slowly, gradually building up speed as you become more proficient. Increase difficulty by allowing the opponent to use slow, straight kicks in addition to the pushes. Then continue the progression by allowing double-handed pushes and circular as well as straight kicks – but always performed at a speed that does not overwhelm the defender.

It is impossible to over-emphasise the value of this type of training drill. It teaches a whole range of essential basic skills without which, all subsequent techniques are of lesser value. Always include these timing/distance/stance drills into your training and you will never be caught out on the wrong foot!

5

DEVELOPING HIGH-ENERGY PUNCHES

INTRODUCTION

This chapter will concern itself with the punching techniques that occupy around 40 per cent of a modern karate training syllabus. Karate's Chinese progenitors – the long hand boxing styles of southern Shaolin – devote around 70 per cent of their syllabus to punches in one form or another. Early Okinawan karate also contained relatively more hand techniques, and used only a few low, direct kicks to the opponent's groin or kneecap. But during the 1960's, syncretism with other martial arts resulted in the influx of high circling kicks such as are found in Korean taekwondo ('Way of the foot and fist').

This influx increased engagement distance between two fighters which, in turn, led to an over-emphasis on long-range punching tech-niques. There has been a corresponding de-emphasis on short-range punches such that close-up engagements in modern karate are typically characterised by the exchange of relatively inef-fective techniques. But it is not that the techniques being used are themselves ineffective; it is just that they are being used from the wrong distance.

This shortcoming has been addressed by free-style karate coaches, with the result that long and short-range punches are now practised alongside each other.

MAKING AN EFFECTIVE FIST

The first stage in developing both a long and short-range high-energy punch consists in learn-ing how to make an effective fist. Do this by open-

Fig 44 **Check the fist profile to ensure that the fingers are properly folded in.**

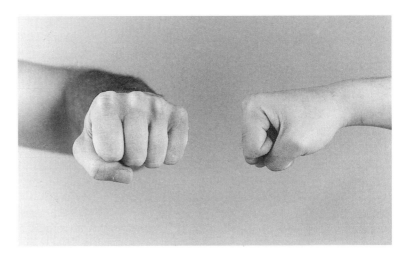

ing out your fingers and thumb. Then curl the fingertips down to touch the fleshy bar running along the base of the fingers. Roll the fingers into the palm, and lock the index and middle fingers with the thumb. Do not enclose the thumb within the rolled fist, since this is likely to result in injury on hard impact.

The second stage is to check the profile of the effective fist (Fig 44). Look first at the angle made by the back of the hand and the folded fingers. This should be close to 90°, so impacts are made on the knuckles and not on the middle joints of the fingers. Though at first the correct profile may be difficult to achieve, it is nevertheless essential – so keep working at it.

The fist is naturally rounded, so it is possible to strike either with the index/middle finger knuckles, or with the lower three knuckles. Classical karate generally uses the former, though there are circumstances in which the lower three knuckles would be a more obvious choice. For

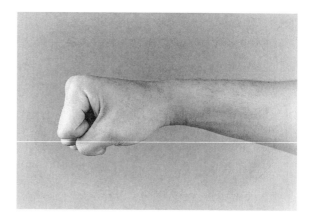

Fig 46   **The bones in the hand must be in line with those of the forearm.**

example, punching upwards leads you naturally to use the lower three knuckles, with the thumb uppermost in the vertical fist configuration (Fig 45): whereas punching upwards with a palm-down configuration requires extraordinary accuracy to avoid hitting the lower finger joints. The other alternative is to use the index/middle finger knuckles in a vertical fist configuration. This, however, requires you to tilt the wrist forward, and so increases the risk of joint injury.

Fig 45   **Use vertical fist when punching upwards.**

Getting The Correct Wrist Angle

Whichever fist configuration you use, the angle of your wrist is very important. High-energy punches land with considerable force and can cause painful flexing if the fist is not held correctly. Punches using the middle and index knuckles require the supporting bones of the hand to be in one line with the bones of the forearm (Fig 46). This means that the fist should neither droop on the wrist, nor should it lift so the middle finger joints are presented. The two selected knuckles should lead, and the fist should not be angled to one side or another.

Set your wrist joint up for vertical fist configuration by resting the forearm on a flat surface, with the little finger edge of the fist down. Then lower the wrist until it contacts the surface. This sets the correct angle for the lower three knuckles to make safe impact. Check also that the back of the fist is in line with the forearm.

Making The Fist As Dense As Possible

The third requirement of an effective punch is that the fist should be as dense as possible. The object is to make your fist so heavy that even a light blow feels like one from a sledgehammer.

To understand the importance of a dense fist, roll your fingers tightly around a short piece of wooden dowelling. This gives a more solid feel to the punch and even light impacts seem more effective. Duplicate this effect by spasm-closing your fist as it is about to hit the target. Clench the whole fist as tightly as you can to exclude large air spaces from within it, then relax it immediately afterwards. The faster the muscle spasm, the denser the fist. But don't keep your fist closed tightly all the time because this quickly fatigues the forearm muscles and slows punch delivery.

Producing a fast closure of the fist is only half the battle. The other half consists in limiting muscle involvement to the lower forearm only. It is all too easy to involve upper arm and even upper body muscles in the spasm-closing action and if this happens, then the shoulder and elbow joints lose their resiliency and punch delivery becomes stiff and jerky. Remember, a high-energy punch depends upon two factors, the first of which is that the involved muscles contract explosively. The second is that all the uninvolved muscles remain relaxed, so their tension doesn't get in the way.

Begin by clenching your fist tightly. Then alternately bend and straighten your elbow joint as quickly as possible. Keep practising until the forearm muscle contraction used to close the fist does not interfere with the extending/flexing elbow.

The timing of spasm-closure must be correct, and I will discuss this after we have looked at the punch delivery systems.

Training Drills To Develop The Correct Fist Profile

Having described the necessary theoretical conditions for making an effective fist, the next stage is to see how this can be achieved through practice drills. The first drill enables you to form the correct fist profile, so the fingers close properly and

allow impacts to be made correctly on the knuckles

The floor-mounted punching post, or *makiwara* is better than those which attach to the wall because it is more springy and has a greater degree of 'give'. Choose one which is wide enough comfortably to span your fist, and then half as wide again, so the need for accuracy isn't critical. The top 15 cm or so should be padded with a single thickness of the type of synthetic rubber which is used to make conveyor belts. This, in turn, should be covered with a tough plastic sheath that is easy to keep clean.

Traditional punching posts use rice straw bound tightly around the top, but there is no reason why we should not reap the benefits of modern technology when it is available to us. Besides which, rice straw is difficult to keep clean and repeatedly smashing skinned knuckles into it can grind bacteria into the unprotected flesh.

Begin training with light impacts only because the correct training effect is gained from punching the pad over a long period with lower impact blows. Stand with your left foot to the side of the

Fig 47 **Thrust your fist out with the palm turned downwards.**

post and extend your left hand. Pull your right fist back to your ribs. Turn your hips three-quarters away from the post. Pull back your left hand, twist your hips towards the post and thrust your fist out with the palm turned downwards (Fig 47). Aim to strike through the pad, relying on the makiwara's natural spring to bring your fist to a stop. Withdraw your fist to recock the punch for the next delivery.

Try and do about twenty good punches, then switch stances/fists and begin again. Do as many repetitions as time and your knuckles allow, returning to the makiwara each time there is a suitable break in other training.

If you bruise your knuckles, then stop training until the swelling has gone down.

Massage your knuckles after each session on the punching post, using a proprietary cold cream that vanishes into the skin and soothes it. Use an embrocation if your knuckles become bruised or achy and rub this well in. Then clean your hands thoroughly to avoid transferring remnants of the rub to eyes etc.

After only a few such sessions, your fist will form the correct shape and you will automatically position your wrist to the correct angle.

One final point: never, ever neglect *makiwara* training! It is an invaluable warm-up for the fist conditioning which follows.

Conditioning The Fist

Obviously it is no use developing a lot of energy if every time your punch lands on a hard surface, you fracture a knuckle. So having learned how to set your fist up correctly, the next stage is to ensure that your knuckles are properly conditioned.

The training drill for this requires two canvas wall bags one hung at chest height, the other at head height. Begin by filling both bags with polystyrene beads of the type used to stuff beanbags. Make sure you pack enough in to fully cushion your blows. It is a good idea to put the beads into a tough plastic bag first and superglue it closed. Then put this into the bag proper. After a while, the beads will compress down and leave the bag half empty once more, so add more as required.

Begin on the lower bag and strike it forcefully

with your index and middle finger knuckles. Always aim to penetrate the training bag and don't be content just to rain heavy blows on its surface.

Work one hand, then the other, landing about twenty hard blows with each. Then move to the higher bag, standing directly in front of it and moving your arms like pistons to drive each fist alternately into the granules. This time strike with the lower three knuckles in the vertical fist configuration (Fig 48). Perform at least twenty punches with each hand.

Your knuckles will become red and sore as they encounter the new covering material and the different target density. Ease this by massaging embrocation into them at the end of each conditioning session. This treatment is essential to maintain smooth and unscarred skin.

After working on the bags for a couple of weeks or so, you will begin to notice that your knuckles become less sore. This tells you that you are ready to begin the next training phase. Refill the bags with sawdust and return to striking them hard. Some knuckle reddening and soreness will return, but massage this away with embrocation.

Continue training until your knuckles become accustomed to the new filling, then pour out 50 per cent of the sawdust and replace it with sand. Shake the bag up to mix the contents and begin again. When your fists can withstand this too, then change to a 100 per cent sand mix and continue. This will normally achieve the desired

Fig 48 **Strike with the lower three knuckles of the vertical fist.**

degree of toughening, but those who wish to go even further can refill the bags with the iron dust that collects around the base of metal forging hammers and rolling mills!

Remember: a gradual programme will provide tougher knuckles in a shorter time than pitching straight into a sand-filled bag at the outset. This is because injuries take months to heal, during which time conditioning is brought to a virtual stop.

The object of all this conditioning is to make your knuckles very hard and more or less equal in prominence. So watch for any individual knuckle becoming more inflamed or sore than the others and readjust your angle of impact until it is shared evenly over all the involved knuckles. Failure to do this will cause one knuckle to enlarge and make subsequent conditioning more difficult. Always allow inflammation to subside before resuming.

Continuous aches in the knuckles are a sign that you are overdoing it. They may indicate the presence of tiny hairline fractures in the bones, some of which cannot be seen, even under X-ray. These are analogous to the fatigue fractures you get with over-stressed metal. Training through such injury can cause a sudden and serious fracture that puts you out of training for two or three months.

Persons under the age of eighteen should not attempt to condition their fists! Continued hard impacts on young bones can damage their growing points and lead to unsightly stunting of growth and/or unnatural curvatures.

LONG AND SHORT-RANGE DELIVERY SYSTEMS

Having learned how to form an effective fist, the next stage is to understand the theory of two quite different high-energy punch delivery systems.

The Theory Behind The Long-Range Punch

The long range punch uses virtually the whole length of the arm. The elbow joint is flexed more than 90° and the fist is held against the hip in the 'cocked' position. The fist then moves from the hip in the direction of the target, and comes to a stop when the elbow joint is almost fully extended.

The punch is therefore accelerated throughout a long movement by the arm and body muscles, so it develops a great deal of force.

Many karateka wrongly believe that the long-range punch develops maximum impact power when the elbow is nearly straight. This is not the case. The amount of muscle power which can be transmitted through a joint is directly related to the angle of that joint. This is because the points at which the muscles attach to the bones on opposite parts of the joint determine the leverage that can be applied at any point in the joint's range of movement. In the case of the elbow, maximum force for practical karate usage is developed between one-third and three-quarters of extension.

The long-range punch, therefore, has quite a depth of field over which maximum impact energy is generated, so you don't require pinpoint accuracy when ranging on a moving target. This effective depth of field is correctly described by the term 'focus'. A correctly focused punch has enough energy to penetrate into the target, whereas striking the target before or after maximum energy has been achieved robs it of its effectiveness.

This is just as well because there is another drawback to using the full length of the extended arm which is that locking the elbow straight repeatedly when punching powerfully against the empty air (i.e. 'unloaded' punching) will cause joint injury.

All long-range punches have an inherent drawback which is that the long movement itself provides the alert opponent with an opportunity to counter it.

Practising The Long-Range Punch

The typical long-range punch begins with a palm-upwards facing fist held on or near the hip. The hips are twisted 45° from forward facing and the leading guard hand extends well forward. It is open and the palm presents forwards (Fig 49).

The punch begins with an explosive movement of the hips. They begin to twist forwards, though at first neither the upper body nor the cocked fist

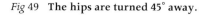

Fig 49   **The hips are turned 45° away.**

Fig 50   **The hips turn forwards but the shoulders lag behind.**

move. This sets up a twisting tension in the spine and when that tension reaches a peak, the shoulders also begin to swing forward and the fist moves away from the ribs. Even so, it lags slightly behind the shoulder movement (Fig 50). This delay pumps up the long muscles in the sides of the body, so they add their power to the developing punch (remember elastic strength?).

Both shoulders move together, so even as the punching fist begins its outward journey, the guard hand begins to withdraw.

At half-way point, the guard hand and punching fist pass close by each other (Fig 51). The punching fist is still rotated palm-upwards and the guard hand is just beginning to close into a fist. The elbows remain close to the sides of the body, so the punching action does not degenerate into a swing.

The hips are now virtually spent, having turned fully to the front. The centre of gravity is beginning to move forward over the leading leg in preparation for impact and the shoulders still have a few more degrees of arc to go before their contribution is also used up. Don't overinsert your shoulders behind the punch because this both destabilises the technique and slows withdrawal.

The closing stage of the punching action is reached when the shoulders turn square-on to the front, with the centre of gravity moving forward. This latter action is important because the most effective absorption of recoil takes place when the centre of gravity is following behind the punching action. This slight forward body movement also has the useful consequence of adding a couple of centimetres of extra reach, which can be of real benefit in the action.

Fig 51 **The hands pass each other at the half way point.**

Fig 52 **Both forearms rotate and the hands clench into tight fists.**

Most classical schools rotate the fist to a palm-downwards configuration as it impacts on the target. The withdrawing hand simultaneously rotates to palm-upwards position and both hands spasm into tight fists (Fig 52). Impact is generally made on the knuckles of the index and middle fingers.

Breathe out sharply as you strike the target.

The weight of the punching arm pulls the shoulder joint forward and slightly arches the back. This both stabilises the joint and adds a few more centimetres of range. The elbows literally graze the ribs as the arms move, and the fists should only rotate when they are close to their final positions. For maximum impact, the punch must land slightly to the side of your own body's centre line. Crossing the centre line always reduces the energy of impact! Correct for any

changes in the opponent's position by turning your body.

Novices tend to concentrate on thrusting out the punching hand and ignore the withdrawing guard hand. This makes the dynamics of the punch go awry. Energy is developed as much by the pulling back of the guard hand as by the thrusting out of the punching arm, so the technique must give an equal emphasis to both components.

Train for the correct action by looping your karate belt around a post. Then take up the slack in the belt and pull your leading hand back to the hip. Both arms will now move at exactly the same speed because they are tethered together.

This is the 'pulley principle' of the long-range punch, first described to me by Ticky Donovan O.B.E., national coach of the British team.

The Theory Behind The Short-Range Punch

The second type of high-energy punch delivery system uses only a slight extension of the elbow joint, so the fist travels only a short distance to the target. In some cases, it travels 25 cm or less, so engagement distances are much shorter.

Because the muscles are contracting over a much shorter distance, they are highly susceptible to interference from non-involved muscles. So localising muscle action is an essential component of the powerful short-range punch.

Whereas long-range punches rely heavily on hip action plus the long fibres in the lateral muscles of the abdominal wall, short-range punches use little or no hip action and emphasise instead the role played by the pectoral muscles in the chest.

This change from hip to upper body action means that the fist is now thrown into the target rather than thrust at it. Attempting to thrust the fist out changes the whole dynamics of the punch and the rigid arm which results is unable to absorb the recoil of impact.

Short-range punches do not necessarily involve the whole body and specialised stances. This means they can be used from a variety of positions, such as sitting, or standing to the side of the opponent. Even so, maximum energy is always generated when power is channelled through the body's own centre line.

Short-range punches have a shallower effective depth of field, but they begin closer to the target and so are more difficult to counter.

Practising the Short-Range Punch

The short-range punch begins with both arms held well forwards, each to its own side of the body's centre line. The hands are open and one slightly leads the other. The shoulders are relaxed (Fig 53). Begin the punch with a violent combined contraction of the upper arm muscles and the pectorals on your chest. This shoots the shoulders forward, and your back becomes rounded, though you must never lead with your chin. The elbow straightens explosively and the punching hand closes spasmodically into a vertical fist (Fig 54).

Initially the fist tilts downwards on the wrist as it travels forwards, but then, as the elbow extends further, it rocks upwards with a co-ordinated wrist/elbow action that helps it penetrate deeply into the target.

Though the arm typically extends fully during unloaded punches, this tends not to happen in practice, where use is made of between two-thirds and three-quarters of elbow movement to ensure maximum energy of impact. In any case, preventing the arm from straightening fully makes it slightly easier to snap the spent punch back, since a fully extended elbow joint presents a mechanical barrier to the elastic action of the muscles. And, of course, not fully straightening the elbow helps prevent injury to the joint.

Inject additional energy by moving your centre of gravity behind the punch. Either slide the leading foot forward, or lift your hips forward and up. A small swivelling action on the balls of the feet can add a further useful bonus of energy.

Though the classic short-range punch makes no use of hip or pulley actions, there is no doubt that such actions do increase the energy of impact. However, if you decide to use them, take care not to turn your centre line away from the opponent, because doing so can prove very risky indeed at the short distances involved.

TIMING THE PUNCHING ACTION

This follows an earlier section in this chapter which dealt with making your fist as dense as possible. We couldn't go straight on to timing the punching action at that time, because we did not then know how to throw high-energy punches. But now we know – here goes!

The punching fist does not close tightly until quite late in the punching action, but that is neither to say that it is ever loose, nor that the wrist is weak! Both of these are serious faults which can cause wrist or hand injuries when the target proves closer than was anticipated. On the other hand, sustained contraction of the forearm muscles early on will slow the punching action and lead to fatigue. Maximum fist compression, and hence density, comes from a very short-lived

Fig 53 **The shoulders are relaxed and one hand leads the other.**

Fig 54 **The fist is thrown at the target and tightens sharply on impact.**

spasm, so correct timing is essential in both delivery systems.

Practise your timing by means of an impact pad held against the partner's chest or upper arm. For those karateka who have never seen an impact pad, it consists of several layers of closed-cell plastazote foam sandwiching a softer, central layer. Even repeated high-energy punching produces no more than a slight reddening of the knuckles and the fact that a man-mass is actually holding it accustoms you to a realistic recoil. Begin by getting the feel of the pad. Just throw your fist at it and don't worry too much about the fine points of technique. Leave the muscle spasm until the last possible instant. If you experience difficulty, then slow your punch down until the spasm action occurs at the correct time. Only when this happens can you once more increase punching speed.

Eventually, you will be hitting the impact pad with a fair degree of force, using both delivery systems (Fig 55). This is the time to increase the level of difficulty by having your partner move towards/away from you, so providing practice at ranging on a moving target.

A target mitt is also useful for building accuracy, though lack of true recoil makes it unsuitable for power training. Your partner uses two target mitts, weaving them in a series of figure-of-eight moves while you try to hit each one accurately.

KIAI

I have tried not to use foreign expressions, but from time to time, we will encounter a concept that

Fig 55   Using an impact pad will teach you how to concentrate force effectively.

is best expressed in the native language from which it came. Such a word is *kiai*. This roughly means 'harmony of spirit'.

What underlies the notion of *kiai* is a union between will, or determination, and effort. You are determined that such and such shall be so, and you marshal the necessary energy to achieve it. So *kiai* basically means a union of intention and energy.

Martial artists are not the only ones to use *kiai*. If you've ever watched the tennis at Wimbledon, you can't have failed to notice the sharp grunts often accompanying powerful strokes. The person heaving a heavy weight also lets out a series of grunts, as does someone trying to push-start a car.

Consider any powerful action involving a spasm of the muscles. Almost the whole body locks up with the effort, including the diaphragm – that sheet of muscle separating the lung cavity from the abdominal cavity. This causes us to expel a short jet of air through the voice-box. And if the muscles of the throat are also tense, then this expelled air comes forth in the form of a grunt. Note that it does not arise through the muscles of the chest wall, but from the diaphragm. Consequently it is deep in pitch.

Martial artists often give shape to the sound by forming their lips and mouth cavity to produce a low-pitched and forceful 'EEEH!'. This need not be particularly loud, though it may well be. The advantage of a loud and penetrating *kiai* is said to lie in the warning it gives to your opponent – telling him that you are not going to be a push-over. That, at least, is the theory . . .

My advice is not to bother making your *kiai* intentionally loud. If it happens as a natural result of the power you are generating, then let it happen. The point is that you don't ever need to make a genuine *kiai* – it should just happen and serve to underscore your efforts.

THE BASIC PUNCHES OF FREESTYLE KARATE

In this section, we will take a detailed look at how to use the principles discussed in the first part of the chapter to make effective and practical punches.

Snap Punch

Snap punch is the first punch of freestyle karate. Begin from a fighting stance, carrying the rear fist close to the chin and the forward guard hand well out from the body. Keep both fists on the correct side of your centre line and drop your chin into your shoulder. Remember – your chin and face are vulnerable, so ensure they are well protected.

If you have enough time, allow the rear fist to drift forward slightly just before you punch because this will help make a useful pulley action. Then pull it back sharply as the forward fist snaps out (Fig 56). Let the punching hip and shoulder both swing behind the arm action and lean slightly into the punch – but keep your chin tucked down and out of harm's way. Weight travels forward over the front foot, allowing the rear heel to lift

Fig 56 **Lean into the punch and draw back the non-punching fist to give extra power.**

slightly. Having said that, don't move your centre of gravity too far forward, or you will be forced to take a step. Don't allow your shoulders to hunch up and don't let the punch cross your own centre line.

It isn't necessary to corkscrew your fist on impact, though a quarter turn from thumb up to palm down may add a little extra impact force. Alternatively, you can strike with your thumb uppermost in the vertical fist configuration. But whichever you choose, spasm-close your fist on impact.

Develop accuracy by practising snap punch against a target mitt. Snap punch is generally aimed at the opponent's nose or jaw, so make sure the mitt is held high enough.

Using your shoulders, hips and centre of gravity correctly will allow you to develop a useful, if not conclusive, amount of force. So improve power by training with an impact pad or a light

Fig 57 **Deliver snap punch with a hip-twisting action that takes you out of line.**

suspended bag. Skip-change stances and punch with either fist, the object always being to dig your fist into the pad or bag.

Increase power by combining the punch with a front foot slide, timing things so the slide comes to an end just as the punch makes contact. Punching too early will throw you forward off balance. Punching too late will allow the kinetic energy created by the slide to dissipate. Practise your timing by punching an impact pad held by a partner.

Increase the technique's sophistication by combining the punch with a front foot angled slide. Twist your hips extra strongly as you throw the punch and allow your rear foot to slide around so your body lines up. This has the effect of changing your line with respect to the opponent. Always try to move to his closed side (Fig 57). Snap punch with diagonal slide is also very effective.

Step forward snap punch is not usually seen in serious free sparring, because if range is correct, then the step takes you too close to the opponent. Even so, it may be useful against someone who steps back each time you attack, and you want to overtake his retreat. Hold your guard still as you move, adjusting the length of the step forward to suit the distance you want to cover (Fig 58). Add a slight diagonal component to the step and you may succeed in changing line to your advantage. Don't let your shoulders hunch up.

Provided you didn't change your guard, then you are now well placed for a really powerful pulley action. Aim to strike the target as full weight descends on your front foot. If you stepped diagonally, then the more powerful pulley action makes it easier to twist the rear foot around. Punch over the top of the opponent's guard and into his face.

Step-up snap punch is an ideal diversionary movement because the advancing fist closes off the opponent's view of what you are doing. All he sees is a fist growing larger in his field of vision. Throw the punch as usual, perhaps with a forward slide of the leading foot if range requires it. Then slide your back foot forwards as you are punching, so the heels touch each other (Fig 59). I need hardly point out that this is an unstable stance to be in, so use it only if you are going to follow with an immediate kick off the front leg.

Fig 58 **Step forwards while maintaining your guard.**

Fig 59 **Use snap punch to disguise the step up.**

Reverse punch

Reverse punch is the second of the basic linear punches and, though widely used in classical karate, it is not that effective in the freestyle situation. It differs from snap punch in that it is always delivered with the opposite arm to the leading leg. So, if you are leading with your left leg, then reverse punch is made with your right fist.

Begin in left stance by executing a snap punch as described above. It doesn't matter if you perform a static snap punch, a slide forward, or step forward snap punch as a feint. In fact you could try all three since the eventual aim is for you to be able to use your fists effectively in any combination of movements.

Your fist will concentrate the opponent's attention on the face area, creating a window of opportunity for a quickly following mid-section reverse punch. However, this window remains open only for so long as your fist is approaching the opponent's face, so the longer you leave the reverse punch, the less successful it will be.

Use the pulley effect to withdraw the spent snap punch and thrust out the rear guard hand simultaneously. Allow your rear hip to turn forward, slightly ahead of the developing punch. This will cause your front foot to slide sideways as the stance widens slightly. Your withdrawing fist comes back to the side of your jaw as the reverse punch strikes home (Fig 60).

Don't be afraid to throw your centre of gravity forward as you punch since this adds a great deal of power. Having said that, make sure you don't lead with your chin. Strike with a dense fist in either a vertical or palm-downwards configuration and pull the punch back immediately after impact is made.

Fig 60 **Turn your punching hip forward and draw back the non-punching arm.**

Bear in mind that the opening snap punch uses a narrow stance that will not allow you to engage your punching hip properly. This is why you must slide your leading foot outwards. Only then can your hips turn square-on for the reverse punching action.

It is a very good idea to slide your leading leg diagonally forward as you deliver reverse punch, because not only does this allow the hips to open correctly, it also moves your centre of gravity forward and increases impact power. However, if you do advance the front leg, draw up your rear foot too, so the stance doesn't elongate to the point where it becomes ungainly.

Practise reverse punch as you step back. This is useful for dealing with an opponent who advances into you. Step back from the immediate threat,

changing your guard swiftly and keeping your chin safely tucked into your leading shoulder. Deliver the punch with your rear fist, just as full weight settles on the back leg. Take a longer stance than normal to allow you to 'dig in', but don't lean forward.

When you have succeeded in getting your timing right and can hit powerfully with either hand as you withdraw, then increase technique sophistication by knocking down the opponent's punch as he steps forward. Begin from left stance and change your guard as you pull back. Bring your right hand across in a palm block and reverse punch over the top of it with your left fist, into the opponent's face (Fig 61).

Next, practise advancing reverse punch. Step forward and perform a front snap punch with your leading fist. Pull it back sharply, letting your front foot slide outwards and thrust out a reverse punch to the opponent's mid-section. Alternatively, begin from left stance, with left fist leading.

Fig 61 **Slide your weight back, knock down the opponent's fist and punch over the top.**

Step into right stance, but leave your left fist out (Fig 62). Punch with that fist just as weight descends on your right foot. This is an extremely fast attacking move, though the fist travels a shorter distance and there is virtually no pulley-action to lend power to it. Compensate for this by stepping forward quickly and leaning into the punch – but, again, watch your chin!

Try a double reverse punch in advancing mode. Begin from left fighting stance by throwing a high reverse punch with your right fist. The object, as always, is momentarily to close off the opponent's vision. As I mentioned at the beginning of this section, throwing weight forward lightens the rear foot, so even as your fist is travelling out, you should be picking up your rear foot and bringing it forwards (Fig 63). The pull-back action of your spent right fist not only helps throw the second reverse punch, out it also helps complete the step forward. This happens an instant before the left fist strikes the opponent in the mid-section. The

second punch is especially powerful because it combines pull-back with stepping forward.

Close Punch

Close punch is used in some schools of classical karate, though its full potential is seldom realised. It is a short, hooking reverse punch that thrusts upwards from the hips, digging deeply into the opponent's solar plexus or chin. Impact is made with the palm of the fist facing upwards.

Begin from a short left stance, dropping the right fist down to your hip. Turn your shoulders towards the opponent and drive your fist upwards and into his mid-section. Lift your hips as the punch is delivered and this will make the impact more powerful. Curl your left hand around the back of the opponent's neck and draw his head forwards and down. This does two things. First of all it prevents him from pulling back from your punch and secondly, his face makes an attractive alternative target (Fig 64).

Fig 62 **Step forward quickly whilst leaving your left fist out.**

Fig 63 **Use the punching action to help draw your trailing foot forwards.**

Fig 64 **Pull the opponent's face down onto your punch.**

Note that the punch does not move in a straight line, as did the snap and reverse punch. Instead, it curves slightly, allowing an extra distance for muscular action to accelerate the limb. As always, the punch is made with relaxed shoulders and into the centre line of the body.

Accompany it with a slight forward diagonal slide of the leading foot to change line to your advantage. And, finally, keep the punching elbow close to your ribs so it makes good use of your centre of gravity.

Roundhouse punch

Roundhouse punch is a reverse hooking punch that travels in an arc to reach the target. As with close punch, its circular path means that the muscles can act on the limb over a longer distance. However, unlike close punch, roundhouse punch travels more or less horizontally and is generally applied to the side of the opponent's jaw. The fact that it strikes the side of the jaw makes it very effective at producing knock-outs.

Its curling path also makes it very difficult to block – it has a tendency to curl around the blocking forearm and still hit the target. Sometimes the opponent misreads your intention and actually moves into it, considerably adding to its effectiveness. Use roundhouse punch when the opponent's guard rules out linear punches.

If the technique is ever used against you, step inside the punch and counter with short-range straight punches.

Roundhouse punch uses a similar method of delivery to reverse punch. Begin from left stance and slide your leading foot diagonally forward and out. Twist your hips and shoulders in the direction of the punch and draw back your left fist to protect your chin (Fig 65). Your right fist travels around and into the target, turning palm-downwards as it strikes home (Fig 66). Lean well forward, but don't offer your chin as an easy target. You will find that your upper body turns naturally in the direction of the punch, but avoid turning too much, since this takes your centre line away from the opponent and places you in a weak position.

Roundhouse punch therefore uses both pulley-action from the draw-back of the leading guard hand, and slight forward body movement.

Practise stepping back roundhouse punch, since this is particularly effective against someone who is single-mindedly advancing into you. Use the same sequence of movements as for orthodox reverse punch. Be sure also to practise the punch in its other modes.

Interestingly, this is the only punching technique in which the elbow moves far away from the side of your body during delivery.

MULTIPLE PUNCHING

It is not enough merely to throw your fists willy-nilly at the target. Each punch has to be an effective technique in its own right, so when beginning your training programme, don't sacrifice skill for speed. Begin slowly, making each punch count.

Fig 65 **Step to the opponent's closed side.**

Fig 66 **Swing your right fist around and into the opponent's jaw.**

Use the pull-back of the spent punch to power the following one and always try to sink your blows deep into the impact pad or punch-bag. Get a partner to steady the bag if it begins swinging wildly.

You will find that the corkscrew punches of classical karate have little application here. Instead, strike with fists vertical, palm-upwards facing as in a short hook, or palm-downwards facing.

Once you can hit the bag or pad hard with either hand, then begin moving around it, learning to punch as you move. You will find that fast multiple punches will not allow you to overinsert the shoulders. So turn them only so far as is necessary to dig into the bag with hard, jolting impacts. Allow the feet to swivel freely as your hips see-saw from side to side. Bob and weave as you fire off volleys of punches.

Next, vary the height of the punches, aiming one high at an imaginary opponent's face and the next to his stomach.

When you can hit the bag hard with repeated flurries of punches, then switch to target mitt training. Here the accent is on speed and accuracy rather than on power. Your partner uses two mitts, weaving them in a figure-of-eight pattern as you try to hit both with volleys of punches. Get your partner to move around as your accuracy improves, so you learn how to zero-in on a small and moving target.

TACTICAL PUNCHING

Energy of impact depends upon a number of factors, two of which are acceleration and mass. The smaller and lighter fist must travel very fast indeed to match the energy of impact of a slower moving, but more massive, weapon. In practice, this means that the fast-moving lightweight may have to strike twice or more times to deliver the same amount of energy as a single blow from the slower heavyweight.

So if you are both lightly built and agile, then train to deliver a series of fast punches to vulnerable targets. But if you weigh 90 kg or more and are very strong, then train to deliver a smaller number of sledgehammer blows. In other words, choose the most suitable alternative for your build.

Punching techniques are particularly effective against the good kicker. He needs a lot of space to develop his techniques and by crowding close all the time, you are taking away his advantage. Short-range punches are also effective against the classical karateka because virtually all his own punching techniques are geared towards middle-distance engagements. Also, move in on the taller opponent, so he can't use his superior reach against you.

Never rely upon single punches. Always use at least two, unless the opponent is clearly wide open. Aim at different targets and mix straight jabs with circular punches. Straight punches drive the opponent's head back and make good feints; hooking punches produce the greatest chance of a knock-out.

Put the opponent under constant pressure by keeping up an unremitting barrage of punches. One slip from him is all you need to land an effective punch. Also, your effective and continuous rain of punches will prevent the opponent from attacking you. But for this to work, your attacks must be serious in intent, powerful and dangerously accurate.

Never over reach with a punch. Take a short step to close range, or use a kick – never punch while in kicking range, or kick while in punching range. Use the diagonals and always step towards the opponent's closed side, so he is forced to turn towards you before he can punch.

You can't successfully block someone who is firing volleys of punches at you, so don't even try. Instead, punch through them in combination with a side step, taking his punches on your forearm and knocking them off course even as you counter-punch. No matter how good you are, you will always take the odd hit, so make sure you are tough enough before you begin sparring with someone.

6

DEVELOPING EFFECTIVE STRIKING TECHNIQUES

INTRODUCTION

The distinction between punches and strikes is both very slight, and very difficult to make. In general terms, punches use the fist in such a way that the front of the knuckles hits the target. No strike does this, though one-knuckle fist gets very close. In the latter case, however, it is a finger joint rather than the knuckles themselves which make contact. And it therefore isn't a punch – but it is called one all the same! Very confusing!

Most hand techniques in classical karate are punches, but it was not always so. Okinawan karateka favoured strikes such as one-knuckle fist, knife and spear hand etc., believing that they were an effective way of concentrating impact over a smaller area to greater effect.

Try this little experiment: place your fist against your partner's ribs and push hard as he resists. Next, use one-knuckle fist against the same spot and press hard. You will find that your partner is hurt far more by the single finger joint than he was by the whole fist, even though you used the same amount of pressure in both cases.

Strikes provide a useful and effective range of hand techniques, so they must all be incorporated into the freestyle karateka's toolbag.

ONE-KNUCKLE PUNCH

One-knuckle punch is an excellent hand weapon for the expert karateka. It concentrates a lot of impact energy over a very small area and its results

will surprise you. Use it in the short to mid-range environment.

Accurate targeting is essential! Remember: one-knuckle punch is a precision instrument, so use it only when there is a clear and vulnerable target – otherwise rely on an orthodox punch.

There are three common versions of one-knuckle punch. The first uses the middle joint of the middle finger, the second uses the middle joint of the index finger and the third uses the middle joint of the thumb. The first version is favoured in classical karate styles, though to my mind it is not as effective as the second version. No matter how hard you try to lock the middle knuckle out, it just doesn't have the rigidity that the second version has.

Roll your fingers into your palm, as though forming front fist, but leave the middle finger partly extended. Lock it out by squeezing in on it with the index and fourth fingers. Then complete the fist by folding your thumb across the fingers.

Use side-step or one of the diagonal forward slides to set up your attacking line. Then throw the fist into the opponent's ribs, spasm-closing it on impact. The higher on the rib-cage you strike, the more effective the technique will be. Use this version in both linear and circular modes.

Form the second version of one-knuckle fist by closing your fist as before but this time extrude the flexed index finger, locking it out with the ball of the thumb (Fig 67). This version is most often encountered in Chinese martial art systems, where it is sometimes known as 'the phoenix-eye fist'. Experts use it as a short, jolting, linear strike to

Fig 68 **Press your thumb into the side of the index finger.**

Fig 67 **Use the extruded index finger joint to attack the opponent's solar plexus.**

targets such as the opponent's breast bone, though it can also be used for angled attacks when the opponent's centre line has been turned.

The third version uses the middle joint of the thumb. Roll your fingers into a fist and press the ball of your thumb into the middle joint of the index finger, so the thumb joint sticks out to the side (Fig 68). Use it in a circular strike to the opponent's temple or side of jaw.

Toughen the three versions of one-knuckle fist against wall bags and practise for accuracy against a target mitt. Don't forget to massage the joint after conditioning to reduce disfigurement.

HAMMER-FIST

If the last strike was used most effectively by the expert, hammer-fist is the novice's favourite. It uses the pad of flesh between the base of the little finger and the wrist. This is pushed up when the fist is rolled tightly and the thumb locked down across the closed fingers in the manner of an orthodox fist. The pad protects the underlying bones of the hand, though it also, of course, protects the opponent's bones from the force of your strike.

The name 'hammer-fist' aptly describes the way the fist is used in a clubbing action against the opponent's face, head and groin. Hammer-fist is also used by the novice to knock away incoming punches and kicks. It works effectively in both close and mid-range environments.

Hammer-fist achieves its greatest potential with the heavier built martial artist and is at its best when you have doubled the opponent forward. A downwards travelling hammer-fist strike to the base of his skull is then a weapon of choice.

Take up a left fighting stance and extend your left hand well forward. Draw the right back and turn it palm-upwards facing on the hip. Draw your left arm across your chest, with the elbow pointing forward. At the same time, raise your right hand behind your head (Fig 69). Then use a pulley-type action, drawing your left arm back to the left hip, and swinging your right arm up and over the top of your head. Strike down on to the target, with both fists clenching tightly as they come to a simultaneous stop (Fig 70). Generate additional power by bending both knees as the hammer-fist lands. This lowering of body weight adds body mass to an already substantial impact.

Practise a shorter range version of hammer-fist by seizing the opponent's leading guard hand with yours. Use his reflexive pull-back to step up to your front foot. Judge the length of the step up to suit the distance to be covered. At the same time, draw the opponent's guard diagonally down and across his body. This will do two things. First, it will bring his face forward and into range. Secondly, it will close his body off and prevent

him from counter-punching you.

Combine the drawing action of your left arm with a vertical hammer-fist strike to the opponent's nose or temple (Fig 71).

Synchronising these movements for best effect requires practice. Aim to strike the opponent both as your step up is coming to a stop and as your left arm has closed him off.

The third version of hammer-fist assumes that you have started from a weak position, with your back turned to the opponent. Begin to twist towards him, guarding your face with your open left palm and folding the right arm across your body (Fig 72). Rotate the right fist until the little finger brushes your chest. Twist around using hip action, and strike back and down into the opponent's groin (Fig 73).

Some classical styles of karate suggest that you

Fig 69 **Bring your right fist up and behind your head.**

Fig 70 **Strike down on the target.**

Fig 71 **Draw the opponent's leading arm down and across his body, then strike him on the bridge of his nose with hammer-fist.**

Fig 72 **Protect your face with your left hand and fold the right arm across your body.**

turn into a straddle stance, striking out horizontally with your hammer-fist. But a sideways-on stance at such a close range may be even more vulnerable than your starting stance. Secondly, hammer-fist to the ribs is not as effective as hammer-fist to the opponent's groin.

I don't know whether it is strictly necessary to condition hammer-fist, but if you wish to try, then one way is to rest a wall bag on top of a sturdy table or bench and then thump it with repeated hammer-fist strikes.

BACK-FIST

Back-fist uses the back of the knuckles in a circular strike to the temple, bridge of nose or jaw. It

works well at all engagement distances and, like all circular techniques, it is difficult to block. However, it is inherently a weak technique, because no matter how stiffly the wrist is held, it always gives on impact and wastes energy. Even so, it is a fair diversionary strike to use from a disadvantaged position with the centre line turned away from the opponent.

Form back-fist as though making an orthodox fist, but do not close it tightly until impact is about to be made. The wrist joint must be springy, but definitely not loose or floppy.

I now want to consider three effective ways of delivering back-fist. Begin from a fighting stance in which your rear hip is pulled back 45°. First,

Fig 73 **Twist your hips and strike the opponent's groin.**

turn the hips fully into the target using a twisting action of the spine to power the upper body's movement. Let both guard hands swing together, because this helps shoulder action and generates extra power. Lift the punching elbow until it points directly at the target (Fig 74), then lash out with the fist, striking the side of the opponent's jaw with the back of the two large knuckles (Fig 75). Keep your arm totally relaxed until the moment of impact, then tense it. Shift your body weight forwards to increase impact. Note the guarding hand with the fingers extended near the elbow.

The second version of back-fist is favoured by some classical karate styles. It uses only one arm to produce a long range and fairly powerful strike by reversing the delivery mechanism, so the upper body rotates away from the target and the striking arm literally 'unrolls' into it (Fig 76). Lean into the target, relaxing your elbow and wrist until impact (Fig 77). Then tighten the muscles and allow natural joint elasticity to snap the wrist back.

Though a sophisticated technique, this method has the serious disadvantage of turning the body's centre line away from the opponent. This, coupled with the inherent weakness of the technique, inclines me not to recommend this particular version. So far as I am concerned, it is no more than a desperate move to slow the opponent once he has turned your centre line and is coming in for the kill.

The third version of back-fist is a close-range technique using a vertical action to bring the upper surface of the major knuckles against the opponent's nose. Use this from a forward-facing position.

Step up to your front foot as you grab the opponent's leading guard hand and close him off. Then strike him full on the bridge of his nose with a vertical back-fist (Fig 78). A springy wrist action is essential.

Toughen back-fist against wall bags and a suspended punching bag, always aiming for a really sharp impact and an equally fast retrieval.

Fig 74 **Point the punching elbow at the target.**

Fig 75 **Turn your hips and shoulders towards the opponent, move both arms together and strike him in the side of the jaw with back-fist.**

Improve accuracy by working against a moving target mitt held sideways-on to you. Have your partner lift the mitt randomly with the pad facing or turned 90°, from you and switch between snap punch, reverse punch and back-fist, as appropriate.

HALF-OPEN FIST

Half-open fist is a little-used strike in which the fingers are folded only at the middle knuckles. Impact is made on these middle knuckles and the thumb locks against the side of the palm. Use it in a vertical configuration to attack the opponent's ribs, or slip it under the chin and into his throat (Fig 79).

Half-open fist needs plenty of conditioning to make it both safe and effective. It works at all engagement distances, and in both linear and circular modes.

An interesting version of half-open fist is found

Fig 77   Unroll your body away from the strike and lean in to get extra range.

Fig 78   Step up and strike the opponent on the bridge of his nose with vertical back-fist.

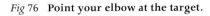

Fig 76   Point your elbow at the target.

Fig 79 **Slip half-open fist through a narrow gap.**

in one classical form of karate, where it looks like nothing so much as a novice's attempt to form a regular fist. Instead of a 90° angle between back of hand and fingers, the middle joints of all the fingers extend forward and make contact before the knuckles. To present them properly, the wrist is slightly lifted, so the joints are in line with the bones of the wrist.

The strike is surprisingly effective when used together with a relatively low-energy throwing or thrusting action.

PALM-HEEL

Palm-heel uses the palm of the hand instead of the fist in both linear and circular short/middle-range strikes. It is an especially rigid weapon, because impact energy is not transmitted through the mechanism of the wrist joint. Like hammer-fist, it uses a pad of flesh to cushion the bones, so less

conditioning is needed. Palm-heel is very effective for those with delicate wrist bones and/or who experience difficulty in making a tight, dense fist.

Form the weapon in two different ways. First, try bending your fingers so the tips brush the pad of flesh running along the top of the palm, as for half-open fist. Then fold the thumb in and flex your wrist back as far as it will go. Try the second way by curling the fingers and thumb forwards and allow them to flex back naturally on impact.

Practise short-range palm-heel by striking against a dense wall bag. The curled fingers brush the bag, then the elbow slams straight, thrusting the heel of the hand forward in a gooseneck action (Figs 80 & 81).

When you can perform this technique effectively, step well inside the opponent's punching distance and, keeping your elbow close to your body, thrust your palm up and under his jaw, driving his head back (Fig 82).

Use palm-heel in a mid-range mode by stepping diagonally forwards to the closed side of the opponent. Swing your right palm-heel up and over his left shoulder, and into the side of his jaw. The attacking palm-heel loops high and then drops down into the target with your elbow slightly higher than your wrist (Fig 83). Increase impact by pulling back the other hand.

CLAW-HAND

Claw-hand is a low-velocity close-range strike. It is unique in that it is what I call an 'active' weapon. Punches and strikes are thrown at the target and cause damage simply by the force of their impact. Beyond being dense, they themselves have little to do with the technique's effectiveness. Claw-hand is thrown at the target and it is only then that it becomes active, the fingers digging into the opponent and holding him firmly. Little imagination is needed to visualise the damage caused to the face by a combination of sharp nails and a powerful grip! But claw-hand can also be used to grip the opponent's limbs firmly while the other hand is used to punch or strike him (Fig 84).

Train for an effective claw-hand by snatching a heavy weight out of the air with a downwards or

Fig 80   **The fingertips make first contact with the target. Note the bent elbow and wrist.**

Fig 81   **Then straighten your elbow and slam the palm-heel into the target.**

Fig 82   **Use palm-heel as a straight jolting thrust.**

Fig 83   **Palm-heel loops over the opponent's shoulder and into the side of his jaw.**

Fig 84 **Use claw-hand to firmly grasp the opponent.**

upwards slashing action. Chinese martial artists use a rough-edged rock, but other dense objects such as weights can also be used. Train for grip with a tennis ball, aiming for a sudden sharp spasm that tenses all the muscles in the lower arm. Be careful not to let this contraction spread up your arm and into the shoulder or it will cause unacceptable rigidity and slowness.

It should not be necessary to grip a person very tightly over longer periods of time, so I do not recommend the isometric training methods favoured by some classical schools. These involve using the fingers to grip and lift heavy earthenware jars.

A different version of claw-hand is no more than an open-handed flick to the opponent's eyes. The action is similar to shaking drops of water from your hand, and the object is to bring your fingertips close enough to the opponent's face to cause him to blink. This creates a window of

opportunity through which a second and more powerful attack can be launched.

KNIFE-HAND

Knife-hand can be used with both circular and direct thrusting actions. Typically it is a mid to long-range hand weapon using the little-finger edge of the palm to concentrate a great deal of force over a narrow strip. Accurate distancing is essential. Use only that part of the hand which lies between the base of your little finger and the wrist.

Press the thumb into the side of your hand, then stiffen your fingers on impact to prevent them from jarring painfully together. Curl the fingers slightly during horizontal circular strikes.

Knife-hand is most effective when applied to the opponent's neck, throat, side of jaw or groin. The throat strike is particularly dangerous because, like half-open fist, knife-hand's narrow profile allows it to slip under the chin.

Step diagonally forward with your right foot to the opponent's closed side, using the movement of your centre line to power the strike. Hook your left wrist over the opponent's leading left guard hand to close him off, and bring your right hand back to your right ear, as though saluting (Fig 85). Allow your hips to build up torsion in the spine, then let the shoulders move into the strike, twisting your hand to a cupped palm-upwards position as it strikes just below the opponent's left ear (Fig 86). Develop additional power by leaning into the strike but don't ease tension in your blocking arm.

The second version is substantially similar except that you step directly into the opponent. Knock his leading guard hand down by bringing your left hand down over it and raise your right, so the fingertips are just above your right ear (Fig 87). Bend your knees slightly to sink your body weight and chop downwards to the base of the opponent's neck (Fig 88). Allow your upper body to turn freely but not so far that your centre line turns away from the opponent.

The third version is delivered when your centre line has become turned away. Look over your right shoulder at the opponent, then open your left hand and bring it forward as a guard hand.

Fig 85 Take the opponent's leading arm across his body and bring your right hand back to your right ear.

Fig 86 Swing your upper body into the strike, catching the opponent with your cupped hand just below his ear.

Fig 87 Knock his leading guard hand down and bring your right hand back.

Fig 88 Chop down at the base of the opponent's neck.

Fold your right elbow and bring your hand palm-upwards facing in front of your left jaw (Fig 89).

Twist your hips back strongly towards the opponent and allow the shoulders to swing freely behind them. Let your arm straighten out and chop backwards at the opponent's neck or throat. Rotate your hand to palm-downwards position just as you are about to make impact (Fig 90). Generate additional force by transferring weight backwards over your rear leg and by moving both hands together.

Not all knife-hand strikes travel in a circular path. You can also use it as a linear thrust to attack the collar bones. It uses the same high-energy delivery system as reverse or snap punch, except that impact is made with the edge of the hand, the fingers pointing vertically upwards (Fig 91).

Fig 89 **Bring your right elbow across your body.**

Fig 90 **Chop backwards at the opponent's throat, turning your hand palm-downwards on impact.**

Fig 91 **Use knife-hand as a thrusting strike to the opponent's upper body.**

RIDGE-HAND

Ridge-hand is a low-velocity weapon that is effective only against the opponent's neck or groin. Weapon shape is the same as knife-hand, except that impact is made with the thumb-edge of the hand. Some classical schools of karate extrude the middle thumb joint (see again one-knuckle fist, above) and call this 'ridge-hand'.

Ridge-hand is delivered with a horizontal or vertical circular action. It is a short to mid-range weapon.

Step diagonally forward with your leading left leg to the closed side of the opponent. Hold your left hand in front of your face to act as a guard. Lean forward and swing your right ridge-hand upwards and into the opponent's groin (Fig 92). No pulley-action is possible, because face guard must be maintained this close to the opponent – but it doesn't really matter in view of the target's sensitivity to the lightest impacts.

The second method also uses a diagonal forward step of the leading foot and a face guard with the left hand. This time, swing your right arm up and around with the palm turned downwards. Impact is made to the side of the opponent's neck (Fig 93). Your elbow must be resilient – not stiff – so the technique can curl around the opponent's guard hand. Follow with a leg reap.

SPEAR HAND

Spear-hand is a low-energy mid/long-range technique that uses the tips of the fingers in a thrusting action.

Extend the fingers and fold the thumb across the palm. Then withdraw the middle finger, so impact is spread over three fingers instead of one. Remember to stiffen your fingers on impact.

Deliver spear-hand with thumb upwards against the solar plexus, palm-upwards against the solar plexus and floating ribs, or palm-downwards against the groin or face.

Palm-downwards strike against the face is particularly dangerous and is delivered in the same way as a snap punch. Turn your shoulders into the action and keep your other hand close to your chin. Throw the spear-hand at the target, using a

Fig 92 Swing your ridge-hand upwards into the opponent's groin.

Fig 93 Step to the side and swing your ridge-hand into the side of the opponent's neck.

Fig 94 Lean forward and thrust your spear hand out on full extension.

Fig 95 **Turn your hips and upper body behind the elbow strike.**

Fig 96 **Bring your elbow up and under the opponent's chin.**

slight pulley-action and lean forward to get extra range (Fig 94). Stiffen the hand just before impact, localising muscular action in the lower forearm.

Spear-hand is largely ineffective against well-muscled targets, unless it is thoroughly trained. Achieve this by repeatedly thrusting your fingers against cardboard boxes, pulling the fingertips into one line, so they don't buckle painfully on impact.

ELBOW STRIKES

Elbow strikes are both effective and versatile mid/short-range weapons. Make impact with the tip of the elbow rather than the forearm, since the former is more effective at concentrating force.

Practise on a punching bag or impact pad to learn how to avoid catching your funny bone.

First method for delivering an elbow strike uses a horizontal action from a short left fighting stance. Twist your right hip towards the opponent as you pull back your left arm. Use this action to clear the opponent's guard out of the way as you bring your right elbow upwards and forwards. Continue shoulder action until your left elbow points forwards. Clip the opponent across the side of his jaw but don't overrotate your upper body in case you miss and need a fast follow-up (Fig 95).

The second method uses an upswinging strike to the opponent's jaw, but unless he is leaning forwards, it will tend to hit his chest on the way. Take up a short left fighting stance and twist your right hip forward. Lift your bent right arm in an

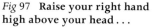

Fig 97 **Raise your right hand high above your head . . .**

Fig 98 **. . . Then drop it down onto the target.**

Fig 99 **Bring your weight back and drive your elbow into the opponent's ribs.**

upwards-swinging arc, so the elbow moves up and into the opponent's jaw (Fig 96). Develop extra force by straightening the knees slightly, so your centre of gravity lifts behind the blow.

Descending elbow strike is very similar to the equivalent version of hammer-fist, since it too drops down on to the back of the opponent's head or neck. Bend your left arm across the front of your chest, turning the palm downwards. Then raise your right fist behind your head and extend it vertically upwards before swinging it forward

and down (Figs 97 & 98). Bend your knees slightly as impact is about to be made.

Use elbow strike if the opponent is standing close behind you. First, look over your shoulder to locate him, then slide your rear foot back a short distance to correct range. Transfer weight quickly over your rear foot and turn your hips towards him. Move both shoulders together and drive your elbow back into his solar plexus or ribs (Fig 99).

7

FREESTYLE KICKING TECHNIQUES

INTRODUCTION

The original kicks of karate were short-range thrusting techniques which used the heel and outer edge of the foot against the opponent's shins, kneecaps and groin. But, later on, these fairly basic kicks were added to from a variety of different sources and they were eventually all but super-seded.

The legs make powerful weapons because they have a large mass and are well supplied with muscles. Provided you have flexible hips and can kick effectively on both legs from shin to temple height, then you have a theoretical advantage over the opponent who can only rely on his fists.

Most kicks are long-range techniques. They can be used from positions where you are quite close to the opponent, though few serious martial artists

would be happy standing on one leg with an opponent in punching range.

Practise kicking on both legs and if you are weaker on one side than the other, then bias your training to equalise skill and power. Finally, it is normally not necessary to condition foot weapons, though you must train to set them up correctly.

We will now examine each of the kicks of freestyle karate in some detail, beginning with front kick.

FRONT KICK

Part Of Foot Used

Orthodox front kick uses the ball of the foot to strike the opponent. This is an effective weapon because it has both a narrow impact zone to focus energy efficiently, and padding to protect the bones of the foot from injury.

Short-range front kicks with the heel are used occasionally to attack the knee or groin. The kick is performed so the sole of the foot leads into the target and the toes either point vertically upwards, or they incline to one side or the other.

Getting The Correct Foot Profile

Train for orthodox front kick by pressing the ball of your foot firmly against the floor, while lifting your heel as high as possible. The instep of the kicking foot must be in line with the shin (Fig 100), whereas dropping the heel causes the ankle to flex

Fig 100 **The instep must be in line with the shin.**

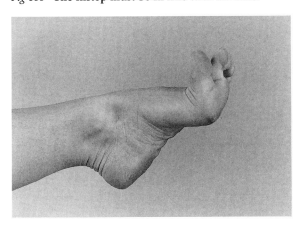

because its bones are no longer lined up with those of the lower leg.

Perform front kick into an impact pad, or into a large foam kicking pad, pulling your foot into the correct shape and stiffening your ankle on impact.

The Theory Behind Front Kick

There are two basic ways by which front kick delivers the ball of foot to the target. Front snap kick uses a fast, upwards diagonal foot movement to give the target a sharp dig. The kicking action is in two parts: the first is an active acceleration phase when the upper leg swings forwards and up. The second is when the lower leg snaps out passively, as though cracking a whip.

Front thrust kick is slightly slower. The kicking knee rises higher than the target, and then drops as the foot extends. This knee dropping action causes the kicking foot to travel more or less horizontally and gives good penetration of the target. Also, the foot is powered all the way to the target and there is no passive phase.

Think of front snapping kick as a precision tool, using a faster delivery with less impact, delivered to a vulnerable area such as the groin. Front thrust kick is more of a sledgehammer.

Performing The Basic Thrust Kick

Begin from fighting stance by changing your guard and twisting slightly on your supporting leg, so the rear hip is drawn forward. Lift the rear foot, but keep the sole parallel to the floor (Fig 101).

Swing the kicking knee forward and up, allowing the supporting leg to swivel a little more. Don't open your groin as the knee rises – bring the ankle of your kicking leg close by the knee of your supporting leg. Keep your elbows to your sides so your arms don't flap about and relax your shoulders so they don't hunch up. The kicking knee swings quickly to the correct height (Fig 102), then it drops sharply as the lower leg thrusts out into the projected mid-line of your body (Fig 103).

Pull your foot back smartly after impact and set it down carefully. Practise the kick in conjunction with a forwards landing or a return to the original starting position, until you can do both with equal skill.

The kicking leg generates a great deal of momentum and tends to pull the body after it, causing the spent foot to slap down heavily in a forward position. Counteract this tendency by leaning back slightly, but always keep the back of

Fig 101 **Keep the sole of your foot parallel to the floor.**

Fig 102 **Raise the kicking knee to the correct height.**

Fig 103 **The knee drops sharply as the foot thrusts out.**

your head in front of an imaginary vertical line rising from the heel of your supporting foot.

Turning the supporting foot during the kicking action increases its range by as much as 25 cm. However, you may not wish to turn your centre line too far from the opponent, even though this means limiting the kick's range. A compromise is probably the best solution, so allow the supporting foot to swivel throughout the kicking action but never more than, say, 60° from forwards-facing.

Powerful front kicks can be made without turning the supporting foot at all. Spring the kicking foot up with a heel-first action and move in a diagonal upwards/forwards path into the target. The back is arched, so it stretches the muscles of the stomach and thighs, causing them to contract more forcefully than in a normal front kick. The hips are also brought up and into the action which, in consequence, is made very powerful indeed (Fig 104).

However, there is one serious drawback and which is that the kick's diagonal flight path makes it difficult to avoid obstructions such as the opponent's knee. Additionally, springing the heel up means that the correct foot shape can't be adopted until well into the kick, with attendant risk of injury.

Another sophisticated way of increasing both range and impact is to allow your supporting foot to be dragged forwards a few centimetres by the force of the kicking action. Raise your supporting heel slightly to reduce friction, and allow your upswinging knee to lift your hips up and forwards. This action provides enough impetus for the drag and your kick gains in range without turning your centre line away from the opponent.

Sliding front kick works well against a heavier opponent, because forward movement helps resist the recoil of impact.

Practice Drills For Improving Front Thrust Kick

Use feedback to make sure that your technique is correct. Your partner can use a padded pole to check that you keep your face back during the kicking action (Fig 105). Turn a chair so its back is towards you and perform a slow kicking action,

Fig 104 **Both hips are projected well forward into the kicking action.**

Fig 105 **The padded pole ensures that you keep your face back during the kick.**

lifting your foot over the chair back and retrieving it the same way afterwards. If the chair back is too high, then turn it and lift your foot over the seat instead.

Training with an impact pad is essential to develop the correct kicking action. Unloaded kicks do not teach you how to cope with recoil, besides which they damage the knee joint. However, the impact pad is a small target, so take care when kicking hard. You may prefer to substitute a larger pad.

When you have achieved a degree of skill, get your partner to move around as you practise your kick.

Performing The Basic Front Snap Kick

Front snap kick is performed in much the same way as front thrust kick. Begin from fighting stance and change your guard quickly, allowing your front foot to turn out slightly as this happens. Bring your kicking knee forward and up until it points directly at the target, then snap the foot out

Fig 106 **Thrust your foot downwards and into the opponent's groin.**

and into the target. Retrieve it smartly afterwards and set it down carefully.

The fastest front snap kicks use very little twist on the supporting leg and there is no need to change the guard if you are not advancing.

Short-Range Front Thrust Kick

Though it is never a good idea to stand on one leg when you are close to the opponent, there are circumstances in which a kick is the only impact technique available to you – for example, when your wrists are being held. In this case, a short-range front thrust kick is the technique of choice.

This technique is delivered with the rear leg. The arms remain stationary as the rear knee swings forward and up. The supporting foot only swivels slightly and the hips thrust forward, delivering the heel or ball of the foot into the opponent's knee or groin (Fig 106). Retrieve your kicking foot as quickly as possible.

You can also use this technique to attack the opponent's knee as you move to his closed side (Fig 107).

Fig 107 **Move to the opponent's closed side and kick the side of his knee.**

Front Leg Front Kick

Front kick can also be performed with the leading foot, though the distance over which the kick can accelerate is much reduced. Consequently, it is less powerful than the rear leg version.

Use front leg front thrust kick to check the onrushing opponent (Fig 108). The deficit in power is cancelled out because the opponent himself supplies much of the impact force. Be prepared to project weight forward, otherwise recoil may unbalance you.

Use the snapping version to attack the opponent's groin. Begin from fighting stance, shifting your weight back over the rear foot and raising the leading knee (Fig 109). Snap kick into the opponent's groin with the ball of your foot and set it down to the outside of the opponent's foot, where it cannot easily be swept.

Front Kick To The Face

When you are reasonably adept at practising the various versions of front kick to mid-section, try front kicking to the opponent's face (Fig 110). This

Fig 109 **Shift body weight back over the rear foot and lift your kicking knee.**

Fig 108 **Check the opponent's advance with a front leg front thrust kick.**

Fig 110 **Front kick to the opponent's face requires good flexibility.**

Fig 111 **Turning front kick is intermediate between a front kick and a roundhouse kick.**

Fig 112 **Use scissors step as an accelerator for your front kick.**

uses the same action as the lower snap kick, except that it requires far greater flexibility in the hamstrings. So don't try this kick until you are sufficiently flexible, or your technique will suffer.

Begin as for the mid-section version by raising the kicking knee until it points directly at the opponent's face. Don't allow the supporting leg to straighten, because the bent knee is better able to control your centre of gravity. The sole of your supporting foot must remain flat on the floor. Keep the kicking knee quite close to your body and don't lean back too far, or recoil will throw you off balance.

Turning Front Kick

Turning front kick uses a lifting action of the kicking hip and a slight twist on the supporting leg to send the foot on a diagonal, lifting path. The technique is intermediate between a front kick and a roundhouse kick, though it is closer to the former. Use turning front kick when the target is partially closed to the normal kick (Fig 111).

Skipping Front Kick

Skipping kicks are a useful way of moving forward quickly and kicking. Skip-change your stance, beginning the kick even as the supporting leg touches down in its forward position. As always, the most difficult part is to synchronise the skip forward with the foot landing on the target. If you kick too early, you will pitch forward off balance. If you kick too late, momentum will be lost. Use diagonal skipping kicks to change line and attack simultaneously.

One-Step Front Kick

One-step front kick makes use of a scissors step, both as an accelerator, and as a means to close distance. Begin from fighting stance by sliding the rear foot forwards while twisting it outwards (Fig 112). Adjust the length of the step to suit the distance to be covered. It is never a good idea to take an undisguised step towards the opponent, so divert his attention with a fast snap punch to his face. Then lift the kicking foot and thrust it into the target. Retrieve the kick as usual and set it down carefully.

No matter how effective the feint used, the step forwards remains a weak link in the technique, so the faster you make it, the greater your chance of success.

Troubleshooting

A common fault is not to use your hips correctly to focus the kick. This shows itself as an upswinging foot movement that skates up the surface of the target pad without penetrating it. Aim to kick into the pad, using a diagonal or horizontal flight path. This means kicking out with the lower leg as the knee is still moving, and injecting your hips into the action. This thrusting action must coincide exactly with the motion of the rising knee, otherwise the kick becomes jerky and power is wasted.

A second common fault is to lose control over your centre of gravity, so the spent kick slaps down. This happens because you have moved your body weight too far forward and the momen-

Fig 113 **Pulling back your front foot before kicking makes you less vulnerable to counter attack.**

tum of your kicking leg has unbalanced you. Keep your body more upright during the kicking action.

If you find that recoil knocks you backwards, then you could be leaning back too far as the kick lands.

Many problems with front kick arise out of collisions between the foot and the opponent's knees or elbows. Avoid these by raising the knee high and lofting the foot over potential hazards. Also, only use front kick when there is a clear target.

Tactical Use Of Front Kick

One of the best targets for front kick is the side of the opponent's upper chest, because this is an awkward area to block effectively.

It is possible to use front kick effectively from quite a short engagement distance. Snap punch into the opponent's face to cause a reflex blink, then pull back your leading foot and perform front kick (Fig 113).

Don't attempt front kick when you are too far away This may cause you to reach too far and lose control over your centre of gravity.

ROUNDHOUSE KICK

Introduction

Roundhouse is a circling kick, used to attack a whole range of targets from thigh to head. Use it when the opponent is standing at kicking range with a guard that obstructs a linear kick. Roundhouse kicks loop around obstacles and can land behind them.

Since roundhouse kick travels in a circular path, it covers a greater distance than linear kicks and so it faces an increased likelihood of detection. On the other hand, it approaches the target from the side and can sometimes slip in unnoticed. Surprisingly, this tends to happen when the kick is travelling relatively slowly. Perhaps the lack of obvious effort, plus a comparatively slow-moving limb approaching from the side, are insufficient to arouse the opponent to violent evasive action.

The most powerful roundhouse kicks are delivered with the rear leg, though it is possible to perform a fairly effective front leg kick to the opponent's temple, jaw or groin.

All the classical forms of roundhouse kick turn your centre line away from the opponent, so always use them with caution.

Part Of Foot Used

One version of roundhouse kick uses the instep – that area of the foot lying between the base of the toes and the front of the ankle. Extend your toes fully, turning them down so they are out of harm's way, and bring the shin and instep into one straight line.

Though instep is a good foot weapon, it does require you to kick with the correct range and angle, otherwise you may strike with the toes instead, forcing them to bend painfully.

You can also use ball of the foot as the impact area. Pull your toes back – as with front kick – but hold your ankle at 90° flexion (Fig 114).

Each version of roundhouse kick can be performed in either instep, or ball of foot mode, so split your practice between the two.

The lower part of the shin in front of the ankle is a fearsome weapon, though some toughening is necessary before you can use it properly. This is the Thai boxers' favourite foot weapon and they use it to good effect against the opponent's thighs, upper arms and head. Try it and see what you think!

Fig 114 **Pull your toes back to strike with the ball of the foot.**

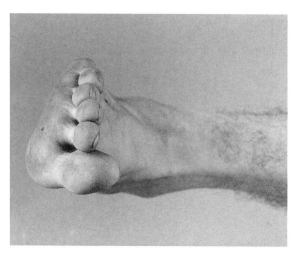

Getting The Correct Foot Profile

Practise getting the right foot profile by kicking a large pad. Your partner holds this against his chest, but if you are developing considerable force, then he can hold it against his upper arm instead.

To practise with instep, kick with a strong ankle joint and don't let the foot flop around. Tighten the foot on impact by extending the toes. Remember, the instep consists of a number of delicate bones covered only by a thin layer of skin. It is therefore vulnerable to injury and should never be used against hard surfaces. Use it instead to attack the opponent's groin, kidneys, ribs and jaw – but watch out for his elbows!

To use ball of foot, pull your toes back on impact and stiffen your ankle. Strike the pad in a horizontal arc or drop down slightly into it.

The Theory behind Roundhouse Kick

Roundhouse kick uses a complicated chain of actions to develop its full impact. In the first instance, power comes from twisting the upper body so the lateral and abdominal muscles are stretched and charged with energy. This is followed by a turning hip action facilitated by the supporting leg twisting outwards. As the kick is being released, so the kicking hip rolls up and over the top of the supporting hip. The lower leg is then powered all the way to the target.

An interlocking system like this requires all the elements to flow together, so acceleration is constant throughout.

Mid-Section Roundhouse Kick Using Instep

The first example of roundhouse kick is one which uses the instep against an opponent's mid section. Begin from left fighting stance, changing your guard but keeping the elbows close to your sides. Bring your right leg diagonally forwards and up. Point your toes and begin to swivel the supporting leg (Fig 115). It will be easier to pivot if you lift the heel slightly.

Maintain smooth acceleration throughout and

Fig 115   **Bring your kicking foot forward and to the side.**

Fig 116   **Swivel on your supporting leg and bring your kicking knee across the front of your body**

bring the kicking knee across the front of your own body. Lean back, so you both counterbalance the weight of your kicking leg and remove your upper body from the likelihood of a counter-attack (Fig 116). Point the knee directly at the target and raise it until the kicking foot is able to travel horizontally into the target. Then thrust the lower leg out (Fig 117). The knee joint acts like a spring, snapping the foot back after impact.

Keep control over your guard, and remain within your own centre of gravity, so you are not obliged to thump down on the spent kicking foot.

Practice Drills For Improving Roundhouse Kick

Any roundhouse kick depends upon hip flexibility, without which the knee cannot be raised

Fig 117   **Then thrust out the lower leg.**

sufficiently. So do not attempt high roundhouse kicks until you have sufficient hip flexibility.

Loft your foot over a chair back and aim for a horizontal, kicking action.

A wall bar is excellent for helping to perfect the kicking action. Stand with your left side against the bar and turn your upper body towards it. Grasp the bar first with your left, then with your right hand. Finally, raise your right foot, flex your knee and bring the ball of foot up and into the wall. If a wall bar isn't available, use the back of a sturdy chair instead (Figs 118, 119 & 120). Aim for the sequential movement of left hand – right hand – kick. This will help you co-ordinate the turning/kicking action.

The next drill is a very strict test of whether you can perform roundhouse kick with skill.

Turn your body into the kicking position and bring your knee across. Then kick slowly and without effort, using only knee action as you lean back. Rest one hand on a chair back if your balance isn't yet quite right, and use a mirror to check technique form. Unskilled students can only perform roundhouse kick quickly; they have to rely on sheer speed to mask errors in both performance and balance.

Roundhouse Kick To The Head

Roundhouse kick to the head is, without doubt, the most common high kick. Perform it as you would the mid-section version, except that your kicking knee must now be raised extremely high. Limited flexibility can be partly compensated for by leaning back – in fact this is advised because it frees the hip action (Fig 121). However, there is something to be said for keeping the upper body more upright (Fig 122). Though this makes great demands on hip flexibility and leaves the body open to attack, it nevertheless produces a fast kick and allows you to follow through without first having to restore the body's equilibrium.

Front Foot Roundhouse Kicks

Perform front foot roundhouse kick from a cat stance by quickly raising the kicking knee to the correct height and pointing it at the target. Your foot is diagonally behind and below the knee. The supporting leg then twists around as the lower leg snaps into the target. The upper body leans away from counter-attack and impact is generally made with the instep.

Fig 118 **Drop your left hand onto the chair back.**

Fig 119 **Turn your hips and drop your right hand onto the chair back.**

Fig 120 **Complete the kick.**

Fig 121 **Lean back to get maximum height.**

Fig 122 **It may be better to keep the body more upright, from which position it can respond quickly.**

The kick's upward curving path takes it around the side of obstacles and into the target, so it is effective when a linear kick is closed off (Fig 123). In your quest for maximum speed, use a snapping action of the lower leg, rather than a powerful thrust.

Sliding Forwards Roundhouse Kick

If your opponent is slightly out of range as you kick, then simply slide a short distance forward on the supporting foot as the kicking knee is rising. Energy for this slide comes from the kicking knee itself.

Drawing Back Roundhouse Kick

Sliding back roundhouse kick provides all the power of a rear leg kick over the shorter distance of a front leg kick. Slide back your leading foot to take your body out of range, then perform a normal roundhouse kick with the rear leg. Disguise the draw back with a snap punch from the leading guard hand.

Step Up Roundhouse Kick

Larger engagement distances can be closed with a disguised skip-change movement. The rear heel skims forward and the leading foot lifts off into a front foot roundhouse kick. Disguise the skip-change with a snap punch to the face.

One-Step Roundhouse Kick

Extend your range yet further with a scissors step past the front leg. Twist the stepping foot outwards as it sets down to set up the hips correctly,

Fig 123 **A high roundhouse kick lifts over obstacles and curves into the target from the side.**

Fig 124 **Use diagonal roundhouse kick to attack the open side of the opponent's body.**

and adjust step length to suit the range requirement. Keep your legs bent throughout so your body doesn't bob up and down, and hold the guard in a relaxed but effective manner. Don't forget to disguise the step with a feint such as snap punch to the opponent's face.

Diagonal Roundhouse Kick

Diagonal roundhouse kick is very similar to the diagonal front kick discussed earlier, except that impact is always made with the instep. An experienced karateka can deliver a very fast kick from his front leg, curving the extended foot around the opponent's thigh and into his groin (Fig 124). The kick can also be used to attack the jaw, though it has a shallow depth of field and tends to hang up on shoulders and elbows. Aim to attack the open side of the opponent's body.

Changing Roundhouse Kick

Changing roundhouse kick is effective for miscueing the opponent and may allow you to kick him quite hard in the jaw without having to turn your centre line too far away.

Begin from fighting stance, bringing the rear knee up and forwards as though you intended performing front kick. The toes, however, point to the floor (Fig 125). Though the opponent realises you are going to kick, he will not be clear at this point which kick you will use. The supporting leg begins to swivel powerfully and the kicking hip lifts only as the lower leg snaps out. This causes a last-minute shift so the foot switches to a rising diagonal arc into the target (Figs 126 & 127).

Train by kicking a target mitt held at the maximum height you can reach comfortably. Kick slowly at first and, as you become more skilled, delay hip rotation until the last instant.

Double Kicks

A good way to train for roundhouse kick is to perform more than one kick with the same leg, keeping the foot off the ground throughout. Begin from fighting stance and use your rear knee for a roundhouse kick to midsection. Pull the foot back after impact, but instead of setting it down, lean back further and raise your kicking knee even higher, so it points to head height. Then twist your supporting foot outwards a little more and thrust your lower leg out for the second kick. This second kick must be performed smoothly, and be withdrawn without loss of balance.

Always kick first to mid-section and then to the head – never the reverse. The reason for this is that roundhouse kick to the head requires a lot of hip involvement, leaving none in reserve for the mid-section kick. The mid-section kick doesn't need as much hip rotation, so it always leaves some in reserve to be used by the head kick.

Trouble shooting

Lack of sufficient hip flexibility is the major problem facing people when they perform roundhouse kick. The average person has trouble raising his knee sufficiently to allow the foot to travel horizontally, so he may be obliged to cheat. Either he fails to turn the hip sufficiently, and the technique becomes a diagonal front kick, or he rotates the hip too far and the knee turns down towards the floor.

Novices lacking hip mobility sometimes extend the lower leg too early in the kick, so the knee is virtually straight and the foot closes on the target through momentum. Unfortunately, straight leg roundhouse kick is difficult to retrieve, so if you use it, then have a follow-up technique in reserve.

If you have problems with hip flexibility during a roundhouse kick to mid-section, then you will find the head kick quite impossible! That is why I strongly advise you to practise the kick to a height which you can manage. If you do that,

Fig 125 **Changing roundhouse kick begins like a front kick.**

Fig 126 **Then the hips begin to turn as the foot nears its target.**

Fig 127 **In the last few instants, the technique turns into a full-blown roundhouse kick.**

then your body will learn the feel of a correct technique and you can simply increase height as your flexibility improves.

Finally, don't swing your knee too far across your body or you may rotate to much and land in a vulnerable position.

Tactical Use Of Roundhouse Kick

Powerful roundhouse kicks turn the centre line away from the opponent, with all that entails. This is something you just have to take into account if you are a lightweight, but heavier karateka can get away with less hip twist and make good use of a diagonal or changing roundhouse kick.

Roundhouse kick is particularly susceptible to line. If your line is bad as you begin the kick, your opponent will be able to slide his front leg forward and reach you with reverse punch or front kick as you raise your kicking knee (Fig 128).

Take even more care when using rear leg round-house kick against southpaws, because no matter how good your line, you are bound momentarily to turn square-on and make a good target. Either draw the front foot back before you kick, or use a step-up version.

If you use roundhouse kick when the opponent is circling you, aim against the direction in which he is moving, so he comes on to the kick and adds to its impact. Don't ever kick in the same direction in which he is circling or you may rotate too much on your supporting leg.

Use a feint to create an attack window through which roundhouse kick can succeed. For example, if you use an effective and powerful reverse punch to the opponent's mid-section, weight will lift off your rear leg. Use this bonus to perform a round-house kick to the head, but time it to make contact just as the spent reverse punch is pulled back.

Confuse the opponent with frequent switch-changes of stance and use the skip-change movement rather than scissors step when you want to close distance.

Fig 128 **Bad line will turn your upper body across the opponent, making a tempting target for the faster front kick.**

SIDE KICK

Introduction

There are two kinds of side kick. One uses a thrusting action to drive the heel deep into the opponent, while the other develops a fast, snapping action. We will consider only the first kind, because the second has very little to recommend it in an actual engagement.

Though an extremely powerful kick, side kick can only be delivered with the body's centre line turned even further away from the opponent than was the case with roundhouse kick. Nevertheless, we cannot always guarantee to be in the correct position with regard to the opponent, and that alone is sufficient justification for practising the technique.

Though side kick is normally thought of as a long-range technique, it can also be used from a very short range indeed – leaving aside for a moment whether it is sensible or not to use a kick from close range anyway.

Part Of Foot Used

Side kick strikes the target with the heel. The foot is positioned so as to present its outer edge, that being the part which runs between the heel and the base of the little toe. Flex your ankle 90° to the shin and lift your big toe, while turning the others down. This may require some practice, but persevere and you will get it. Lifting or depressing all of the toes is an acceptable alternative for novices, but not for advanced grades.

Shaping the foot this way strengthens the ankle and prevents it from flopping around during a hard impact. Pulling the foot back allows the heel to lead and the narrow outer edge wastes little energy when it follows the heel into the target. Don't kick flat-footed because this spreads impact over the whole of the underneath of the foot, with consequent loss of penetration.

Getting The Correct Foot Profile

Train for the correct foot profile with a kicking pad or suspended punch-bag. Keep your foot relaxed, but in the correct shape, until close to the target, then tighten it. Aim always to hit the pad with the heel and not the edge of the foot.

Theory Behind Side Thrusting Kick

Most classical karate styles use a diagonal upwards movement of the kicking foot – the foot starts off from a fairly low position and then travels both upwards/outwards into the target. The body leans away progressively as the kick is in flight and the hips rotate in the opposite direction to the kicking action. This combination of hip twist, and the foot thrusting out, is responsible for generating power.

However, this is not the most effective way to produce a powerful kick. The freestyle method is to lift the kicking foot until the heel points directly at the target. The hip then rolls away from the kicking action as the foot thrusts out horizontally. This produces a much greater depth of field than the classical version.

Short-range side kick strikes with the knee still part flexed – but don't be fooled into thinking it is weak because of this!

Though the hips twist away from the direction of the kick, they also move behind it, sometimes to the extent that the supporting leg is dragged a couple of centimetres.

Side Kick To The Knee

Side kick to the knee is the easiest version to perform and the obvious one to begin with. It requires little hip flexibility, so beginners can learn it early on in their training. Yet, having said that, it has all the components of more advanced versions.

The most elementary form of side kick to the knee begins from a high straddle, or a get ready stance. Shift your centre of gravity over the bent supporting leg by leaning away. Then raise the

Fig 129 **Point your heel at the opponent's knee- cap.**

Fig 130 **Turn your hips away as you thrust your heel out and down.**

kicking knee until your heel points to the partner's kneecap (Fig 129). Thrust your foot diagonally down and twist on the bent supporting leg (Fig 130). Inject additional force by allowing the force of the kick to drag the supporting leg a few centimetres in the same direction. Withdraw your foot after impact, bringing the knee back to your body; then set it down carefully.

Hip action contributes to a powerful delivery, so allow them to rotate freely during the kick. Lean back and don't get your upper body in the way. If you remain upright as the kick strikes, then recoil will jack-knife you forward and you will lose control over your centre of gravity. The action used in side kick from a sideways-on straddle stance involves a drawing back of the leading leg, so engagement distance is actually increased.

Classical karate styles also practise side kick from fighting stance, though front thrust kick achieves the same results with a simpler and faster action. However, for the sake of completeness, a short description of this technique is included.

Begin from left fighting stance and change guard as though performing front kick. This sets up the hip. Then bring your right knee forward and up, drawing it across the front of your body as you pivot on your bent left supporting leg (Fig 131). Lift your right heel and point it directly at the opponent's kneecap. Thrust the foot out and down, using a combination of gravity, hip action and the muscles of the upper leg.

Twist the supporting leg anticlockwise and lean side-on to the opponent. The body leans away from the kick to protect the face and balance properly, and prevents a fall if the kick misses.

Extend your right arm along the length of the kicking leg and flex the left arm across your chest (Fig 132). Pull the spent kick back to the body before setting it down.

Fig 131 **Bring your right knee up and across the front of your body, pointing the heel at the target.**

Fig 132 **Heel thrust out with right arm along the leg, and left across the chest.**

Practice Drills To Improve Side Kick

It is impossible to perfect side kick without practising against a kicking bag – unloaded kicking teaches the wrong weight distribution!

Hold the back of a chair with both hands and extend your kicking foot slowly, while twisting your supporting leg. Draw back your foot and set it down again. This crucial action is very difficult to co-ordinate, and holding on to a chair allows you to concentrate on it without worrying about your balance. Check your technique profile with a mirror.

Trouble shooting

The combination of hip twist, lean back and thrust is difficult to operate concurrently, and novices usually tack one movement to the end of another, producing a jerky, weak action. Continued practice is the only remedy for lack of skill.

If the impact was not as substantial as you had hoped, then check first that you formed the foot correctly so impact was made with the heel and not the sole. Secondly, look to see whether the supporting leg twisted more than 90° from forwards-facing, showing that the hips were properly engaged.

Did you raise your kicking knee high enough, so the foot thrust diagonally downwards from above the target – rather than horizontally outwards from the same height? Did you jack-knife forward on impact, or land heavily on your front foot? If yes, then you didn't lean back sufficiently.

Did the force of impact knock you backwards off balance? If so, then either you didn't project your energy into the kick by turning the hips and sliding into the target, or you kicked with a straight supporting leg. Were you able to set your spent kicking foot down where you wanted, or did it just drop to the floor? If this happened, then you didn't control your centre of gravity.

Side Kick To Mid-Section

Side kick to mid-section is similar to side kick to the knee, differing only in so far as its target is higher. Good hip flexibility is essential, because the knee must be lifted until the kicking heel is at the same height as the target. If the foot isn't lifted high enough, then it must swing upwards to reach the target and this reduces penetration to virtually zero! Therefore, you need the necessary kind of hip flexibility before you begin practising.

Begin from a sideways-on stance and raise your right knee. Lift your big toe and turn the others downwards. Bring the kicking knee diagonally across the front of your body and twist on the supporting leg (Fig 133). Project your hips into the kick as you thrust out the heel, allowing this action to drag you forward a couple of centimetres (Fig 134).

Side Kick To The Face

Side kick to the face requires even more hip flexibility and if you don't have it, then the heel will swing up in a curve and may miss the face altogether. Even though the target is now quite high, you must still use a straight, piston-like action of the kicking leg.

Lean away to help give a direct thrust to the kick, but don't drop your head. Maintain an effective guard throughout and keep control of your arms.

Step Up Side Kick

Step up side kick is an extremely powerful technique which uses the skip-changing movement. Begin from a sideways-facing stance and bring the rear leg over in a low, skimming hop until it lands where the front foot was, just an instant before. As the rear foot is moving, so the front foot is lifting to kicking height (Fig 135). Lean away to set up the kick and turn your hips away from the target as you thrust the foot out. Aim to strike even as weight is settling on the supporting leg.

One-Step Side Kick

The feature of this one-step side kick is that it uses a scissors step. This accelerates the body in the direction of the opponent or target. Stepping behind the supporting leg has the effect of setting the hips to the correct angle for lifting the heel (Fig 136). Then thrust the kick out horizontally.

Fig 133   Turn your hips away from the target.

Fig 134   Allow the kicking action to drag your leg forward a couple of centimetres.

Fig 135   Time the advance so your kicking knee rises as your trailing foot sets down.

Fig 136   Use scissors step to set up your hips for the kick.

BACK KICK

Introduction

Back kick is performed from a position in which your centre line has turned completely away from the opponent. You may need to respond to someone who is immediately behind you, or you may find back kick such an unusual move that it succeeds despite itself.

Back kick is an extremely powerful technique which uses the heel in a direct thrusting action like that of side kick. In fact you would be justified in considering back kick as an extreme form of side thrust kick but one in which the hips have turned completely away from the kick's direction.

Part Of Foot Used

Like side kick, back kick uses the heel of the foot, with the outer foot edge as a subsidiary impact area, so pull the ball of your foot back and allow the heel to project.

Theory Of Back Kick

Basic back kick is a powerful thrusting kick. The movement is entirely linear and relatively uncomplicated.

Spinning back kick is far more complex and uses a combination of rotational and linear movements. Failure to co-ordinate these produces a slow and inaccurate kick.

Body rotation both augments the kick and draws it back afterwards, so you must kick during rotation – not once it has stopped. The faster you spin around, the faster the kick can be performed and then pulled back.

A Basic Version Of Back Kick

Basic back kick begins from fighting stance with the opponent standing directly behind you. Lean forward and look quickly over your shoulder, bringing both elbows close to your sides (Fig 137). Pick up your leading foot and thrust it backwards so the heel leads (Fig 138). Your foot travels back horizontally and the heel strikes the opponent in the groin (Fig 139).

Fig 137 **Look over your shoulder at the target.**

Fig 138 **Pick up your leading foot and . . .**

Partly withdraw the spent foot and set it down in front of, and to the side of, the supporting foot (Fig 140). Then spin around and take up an effective fighting stance facing the opponent.

More flexible karateka can back kick to the opponent's face but this is a small target compared to the mass of the body, and is easily missed.

Practice Drills To Improve Back Kick

A mirror is an essential training aid. Stand sideways-on and look closely as you perform the technique. Check that your head is raised, your elbows are close to your sides and your back is arched.

Improve accuracy by kicking a large pad (the impact pad is too small).

Spinning Back Kick

Face the opponent in left fighting stance. Twist your hips strongly and draw your front foot diagonally back and inwards, where it can take the weight of the body (Fig 141). Turn your back

towards the opponent, but twist your head quickly to look over your right shoulder, so you lose sight of him for the shortest possible time (Fig 142). As your eyes fasten on the target, lift your right foot and thrust it out in a straight line, the heel leading.

Pull the spent kick back against the body and continue twisting until you face the opponent once more. Set your foot down and take up an effective guard.

The first part of the turn consists of twisting on the rear foot while drawing in the left. This involves transferring weight over the right leg, so the left is free to slide. You can therefore speed up this first part of the kick by beginning from a cat stance in which body weight is already polarised over the rear leg.

Once your left foot has been withdrawn by the correct amount, then it is time to shift weight over it so the right is free to lift. In practice this requires only a small adjustment in centre of gravity, because your feet are already close together. The remainder of your turn now takes place on the supporting left leg, so lift the heel slightly and allow the foot to turn.

Fig 139 ... **Thrust it back heel first into the opponent's groin.**

Fig 140 **Partly withdraw the spent kick and set it down ready for a fast turn about.**

Fig 141 **Draw your front foot back and inwards.**

Fig 142 **Twist sharply around until your back faces the opponent. Look over your shoulder.**

Trouble shooting

If you fail to draw your left foot close enough to the right, then the shift in centre of gravity will be more pronounced, and less experienced karateka will experience difficulty keeping their balance.

If you do not turn your hips sufficiently, then the kick will be to the left of centre. If you turn too much, the kick will go right of centre. Limit inaccuracy by using visual feedback to tell you where the target is, and where the kick is headed.

A complete turn brings you to a full-facing position, instead of at a disadvantageous angle to the opponent. Set your foot down in the correct position, or the new stance will either be too wide, or too narrow.

Beginners sometimes hook the heel upwards. Remedy this by practising against a large foam pad.

A Second Basic Version Of Spinning Back Kick

I now want to discuss a variant of the above kick, using a side-step of the front foot, rather than drawing it back. This change in the opening sequence completely alters the characteristics of the kick, resulting in a strong body follow-through and longer range.

Begin from fighting or cat stance. Slide your front foot across the line of the back foot (Fig 143) and twist your hips so your back faces the direction in which you want to kick (Fig 144). Swivel your head quickly to keep your eyes on the target and thrust your right foot in a rising diagonal from the floor to the target. Lean away from the kick and hold your head up to maintain balance. Keep your elbows close to your body. Drop the spent foot to the floor in the correct position for a new

Fig 143 **Slide your foot across the line of the back foot.**

Fig 144 **Turn your hips sharply and look over your shoulder.**

fighting stance and continue twisting until you face the opponent.

Slide your leading foot across by the correct distance or your kick will be off-centre. A rule of thumb is to cover an equal distance on either side of the stance centre line. As you become more skilled you will discover that the step across – swivel – kick movement smoothes into a continuous flow of movement. And it is only when you have reached this stage that you can use this particular version of back kick in a sparring situation.

Comparing The Two Basic Kicks

In the first version, the kick is delivered from a lifted foot flexed knee position. It is therefore a horizontal thrust powered by knee extension and hip rotation. Beyond this latter rotation, there is no body involvement. The second version begins

the kicking action proper, with the right foot resting lightly on the floor in a forward position. There is, therefore, a greater distance over which to accelerate the heel, though this advantage is not gained without penalty. Its diagonal path is all too prone to hang up on the opponent's knees, whereas the first version lifts over them.

Also, the second version shifts bodyweight over a greater distance and in the direction of the kicking action: the kick is more powerful. The longer the starting stance, the greater this body movement, and more body movement, gives range. So, allow for increased penetration when setting up the distance to be covered.

Developing the Spinning Back Kick

Both basic versions use an unnecessary opening movement of the front foot. More advanced spin-

Fig 145 **Bring your back leg forward and across the front of your leading right foot.**

ning back kicks begin from a narrower stance. Just spin around on the front foot as you lift the rear leg and take it across the back of the supporting leg. The supporting leg continues swivelling as the kicking foot extends.

Though this is the fastest method, it is also the most unstable, and requires both skill and speed to operate it correctly.

One-Step Spinning Back Kick

Begin from, say, a right fighting stance, bringing your rear leg diagonally forward and across the front of your leading right foot (Fig 145). Don't stop at this point! Twist sharply on the left foot and turn your head to look over your right shoul-

der. Hold your elbows close to your sides as you perform back kick with your right foot, setting it down in the usual manner afterwards.

This particular version covers a lot of ground and generates considerable power — but it also provides the skilful opponent with a rather obvious cue!

Tactical Use Of Back Kick

Back kick has a very great depth of field. It is effective even if the opponent closes on you during kick execution. It is also effective if the opponent pulls back — because it just seems to keep on extending.

Back kick is best used when the opponent is standing immediately behind you. Other than that, use spinning back kick as a novelty; as an unexpected response, perhaps, to being crowded by a stronger but less skilled opponent. Mask the kick with a powerful reverse punch into the opponent's face. The kick may then possibly slip in under his lifted guard.

Alternatively, use spinning back kick against an opponent who quickly retreats from your attacks and out-distances your flurry of punches. In this case, use a long-range roundhouse kick to drive the opponent back, while focusing his attention high. Then drop the spent kick in a forward diagonal position that allows you to cover a great deal of ground with the following back kick. Be ready with a back fist or reverse punch as you come out of the second kick.

Since spinning back kick is inherently slower than, say, a front-kick, it should always be used as part of a combination technique.

REVERSE ROUNDHOUSE KICK

Introduction

Reverse roundhouse kick is a spectacular technique in which the foot hooks back into the target, using opposite hip rotation to that used in roundhouse kick.

The kick is not particularly practical because it combines all the worst features of back kick with the standard drawbacks of circular kicks.

There are two basic types of reverse roundhouse kick – the front and the rear foot versions. Front foot reverse roundhouse kick uses only a few degrees of body rotation sacrificing power for speed and a short flight path.

The rear foot version is so powerful that it is easily capable of smashing the opponent's guard to one side and carrying on through to give him a resounding thump on the temple. It is so powerful because it uses no less than 180° of full body rotation to accelerate the foot.

Part Of Foot Used

Both versions of reverse roundhouse kick strike with the heel, but when practising against target mitts, the sole of the extended foot is used instead.

Front Foot Reverse Roundhouse Kick

Front foot reverse roundhouse kick relies on a skip-change disguised by a snap punch to the opponent's face. Begin from fighting stance by skimming forward with the rear foot. At the same time, pick up your kicking knee and bring it forward as though performing side thrust kick (Fig 146). Swing your foot out in a shallow arc to the side of the opponent's head, swivelling on the supporting leg in such a way that the foot turns in the opposite direction to the kick. This action unrolls the kick and opens the hips.

Hip action is responsible for powering the kick. The knee plays only a small part, and the final hooking action should not be overemphasised. Flex the knee just enough to hook the heel back and into the target (Fig 147). Lean back to counter the weight of the kicking leg and maintain an effective guard throughout. Retrieve the spent kick as though it were a side thrust kick.

Allow your supporting foot to swivel freely, otherwise the hips will not open out and the technique will change into a reverse crescent kick.

Failure to balance the kick shows itself as a heavy landing on the spent foot, and a poor stance that is wide open to foot sweep.

Avoid the tendency to hunch up your shoulders as you kick and keep your elbows pressed lightly to your sides. Work at the sequence until

the skip – lift-off – kick sequence smoothes out.

If you experience a problem in opening the hips sufficiently to achieve the necessary height, then practise the kick at a height you can comfortably manage and get the feel of a technically correct action. Then increase the height of the kick as your suppleness programme begins paying dividends.

Actually, the kick does not make serious demands on hip flexibility in the way that a side kick does because the kicking leg is moving backwards as well as upwards.

Some karateka try to use reverse roundhouse kick in a withdrawing mode, as the opponent advances into you. This entails drawing back body weight over the rear leg and bringing the two feet together. The kick is then performed with the front foot.

I do not recommend this for three reasons. First, it involves standing on one leg as the opponent advances strongly into you. Secondly, it entails

Fig 146 **Bring your foot forward as though performing side thrust kick.**

turning your centre line away when you can least afford to. Thirdly, it is a very weak kick. You would be better advised using hand techniques in conjunction with a change in line.

Practice Drills To Improve Reverse Roundhouse Kick

Use a mirror to check that the kick has good form, and a kicking bag to confirm both that your foot is configured correctly and that you can strike relatively hard without overbalancing. Train for accuracy with a target mitt, but use the sole of your foot as impact area.

Rear Foot Reverse Roundhouse Kick

The first version of rear foot reverse roundhouse kick begins from fighting stance with an outward twist of the leading foot as the rear knee is brought forwards and up (Fig 148). Until this stage, the

technique could easily be mistaken for a side thrust kick. However, when the knee is raised high enough, the hips open out and the leg extends and curves back in the same way as was described above (Fig 149).

This version is actually much more difficult than the front foot kick, because there is no opening step in which to set the hips up correctly.

The second way of performing rear foot reverse roundhouse kick uses full body rotation. Begin from left fighting or cat stance and twist your shoulders strongly so a torsional stress is set up in the spine. Allow this to build to a peak, then let the hips begin twisting, so your back turns towards the opponent. Slide your front foot back and inwards until the two feet are virtually side by side.

Continue turning your body and pick up your right leg, swinging it diagonally backwards and upwards. Body rotation then wipes the heel across the target. Begin pulling the spent kick back as soon as you can – don't allow a wide and unneces-

Fig 147 **Swing the foot high and hook it back into the target.**

Fig 148 **At this stage, the technique looks a side thrust kick.**

Fig 149   **Then the foot hooks back into the target.**

sary follow-through. Finish by bringing the kicking knee back against your chest, while maintaining an effective guard. Then set it down carefully.

This technique depends upon smoothly accelerating body rotation until the foot makes contact with the target. Keep your eyes on the target at all times by turning your head, and lean away from the extending kicking leg to maintain balance. The kicking leg is virtually straight, with only a slight bend at the knee joint. Adjust range accurately by extending or flexing the knee joint as required. The kick is uncontrolled, so if you miss the target, your foot will carry on round past it. Attempting suddenly to check the kick can jerk your body upright and pull you forward off-balance. So, be prepared to allow a follow-through but, as I said above, don't make it too expansive.

A further version of this kick uses a front foot slide-across rather than drawing it back and in. As with spinning back kick, this causes a major shift in the centre of gravity and extends the kick's range by the length of your opening stance – but it makes it more difficult to control.

One-Step Reverse Roundhouse Kick

Perform a one-step reverse roundhouse kick just as a one-step back kick: step across your lead foot to twist the hips, but keep your stepping foot close to the supporting leg to maintain balance.

Tactical Use Of Reverse Roundhouse Kick

Reverse roundhouse can be used after any technique that relies upon turning the hips. Open with a strong roundhouse kick to the head, leaning well away and allowing the kick to follow-through past the point of impact. Drop the spent foot close to your supporting leg and you will find that your hips are already turned three-quarters away (Fig 150). Simply continue the turning action and lift your supporting foot into a reverse roundhouse kick.

Fig 150   **Land in such a position that your hips are already part-turned.**

Fig 151   **Raise the kicking foot high before dropping it down onto the target.**

AXE KICK

Introduction

Axe kick is both spectacular and powerful, combining as it does muscle power, the weight of the extended leg and the force of gravity to drop the heel on to the opponent's head or collar bones. But it is virtually impossible to control, so take great care when training with a partner.

Axe kick doesn't take your centre line away from the opponent, so your fists remain on-line throughout and ready for immediate use. But it also means that the kick has a shallow depth of field. Increase range by using a skip or drag forwards on the supporting leg.

Axe kick has a clear 'signature'. The foot must rise above the target and then drop down onto it, so your technique can be recognised quite early on in relative terms.

Axe kick involves rather more than a simple swing up/drop down action. If it were, then you would have as much chance of catching the opponent on the upswing as on the downswing. Avoid this by swinging the foot outwards as well as up. Project the kick into the opponent by thrusting the hips forward asymmetrically, so the kicking hip leads.

Part Of Foot Used

Flex your ankle strongly so the ball of the foot is pulled back and points upwards. Pull back your toes and land on the target with the heel of the foot. But don't use your heel in the training hall – land with the sole of your foot instead. This means extending your ankle and turning the toes downwards.

Vertical Axe Kick

Vertical axe kick is the most common version. Begin from fighting stance, bringing your back leg forwards and swinging the foot as high as possible. Allow the knee to bend slightly but then straighten it as it approaches full height (Fig 151). Pull the foot into the correct shape and maximise range by arching your back and thrusting the hips forwards – but don't lean back too far. Then drop the kicking foot vertically on to the target. Beware of dropping your heel unchecked on to a hard floor – this is extremely painful!

Diagonal Axe Kick

Diagonal axe kick is a less common version. Perform it in much the same way as the previous kick, except that the kicking leg rises diagonally upwards to either side before dropping at a slight angle.

Trouble shooting

Axe kick makes substantial demands on the hamstrings. The ballistic swinging action generates a great deal of momentum which can, in the case of less flexible students, cause muscle or tendon damage. Be aware of this and only practise the kick when you have the requisite flexibility.

If you find that your kicking knee bends during the kick it could be that your hamstrings are too tight. Lack of flexibility also pulls the supporting leg straight and sometimes lifts you on to the ball of the foot. There will also be a pronounced tendency for your shoulders to hunch up and/or your elbows to move away from the ribs. Watch for these faults by training in front of a mirror.

Practice Drills For Improving Axe Kick

Train for accuracy, range and correct profile with an impact pad, but make sure your partner holds it by the straps and well away from his body. A firm grip on the straps is essential!

Tactical Use Of Axe Kick

Use axe kick as part of a combination, driving the opponent backwards with front thrusting kick delivered from the rear leg. Drop the spent foot in a forward position to set up the range, then swing your back leg up in an axe kick.

THE CRESCENT KICKS

Introduction

The two crescent kicks travel a circular path, but they score over a roundhouse kick in that they involve less turning away of the centre line. They do not rely on knee extension to generate impact, but use the full mass of the leg instead. However, this makes the kick ponderous, difficult to control and retrieve.

Part Of Foot Used

Crescent kick uses the inside edge of the foot – on the big toe side. Reverse crescent makes use of the outside edge, or little toe side. Foot shape is the same for both, with the big toe raised and the others turned down. The ankle is fully flexed and the ball of the foot points upwards. Practise the correct profile by swinging your foot into an impact pad.

Crescent Kick

Practise crescent kick from fighting stance by turning your shoulders slightly in the direction of the kick. Allow the hips momentarily to lag behind, so the spine muscles are taut. Release the hips, lifting your rear foot and swinging it around with the big toe side leading (Fig 152). Flex your knee at first, but allow centrifugal force to straighten it as the kick develops. Your foot describes a rising arc that 'wipes across' the opponent's jaw (Fig 153) and past it – but not too far. Flex your knee and pull the foot back quickly. The supporting knee remains bent.

Fig 152 **Lift your kicking foot and bring it forwards.**

Fig 153 **Wipe your foot across the opponent's jaw with the big toe-side leading.**

Fig 154 **Take your kicking foot diagonally across the front of your body.**

Fig 155 **Then change direction and bring the little toe-side of the foot into the opponent's head.**

Reverse Crescent Kick

Reverse crescent kick also begins from fighting stance. Once again, the back foot is lifted and brought forwards. However, in this case the knee is slightly bent as the foot travels diagonally across the front of the body (Fig 154). Then the foot changes direction and cuts back into the opponent with the little toe edge leading (Fig 155). The hips open as the foot travels back across the body, so beware of presenting the opponent with a clear target. And don't let the foot travel too far. Bring it up short by flexing the knee suddenly.

This technique shares similarities with diagonal axe kick, except that its major plane of movement is horizontal rather than vertical.

Spinning Reverse Crescent Kick

Spinning reverse crescent kick is often confused with the full reverse roundhouse kick, though an expert can tell them apart simply by looking at the foot shape and the upright body.

Begin from fighting stance by drawing your front foot diagonally inwards. Turn your head quickly so your eyes leave the target for the shortest possible time and continue body rotation. Lift your kicking foot and sweep it across the front of your body (Fig 156). Then flex your knee to draw in the spent foot. A smooth, seamless acceleration is essential for the success of this rather difficult kick.

Perform stepping forward spinning reverse crescent kick in the same way as stepping forward reverse roundhouse kick – except, of course, for the different foot position and upright body.

A SUMMARY OF THE POINTS CONNECTED WITH TACTICAL KICKING

Never kick when in punching range, or if the opponent constantly charges in.

Fig 156 **Lift your kicking foot and sweep it across the front of your body.**

Standing on one leg is never a good position to be in, so perform all kicks as quickly as possible and always maintain an effective guard.

Never kick unless there is a clear target.

Some kicks open your body to counter-attack during the early stages of delivery, so always adopt the correct line.

Kicks which turn your centre line completely away from the opponent make you extremely vulnerable, so use them only when it is safe to do so.

Maximise the chances of success of any kick by disguising its signature until the last moment. Do this by means of feints that divert attention elsewhere, or by using a neutral opening sequence.

The depth of field of linear kicks is difficult to estimate and sometimes the opponent fails to step far enough back. Circling kicks tend to curve further across than was anticipated and sometimes curl right around the opponent's guard.

It is true that kicks delivered with the front foot have a shorter distance to travel but, with few exceptions, they are less powerful. Though slower in terms of delivery, rear foot kicks are much more powerful and, provided you can disguise them, they make the best options.

Snapping kicks use less body commitment and are correspondingly less effective against the more heavily muscled opponent – unless you catch him in the groin. Unfortunately, thrusting kicks which rely on body involvement to generate power are usually difficult to retrieve quickly after use.

In general terms, the lower the target, the more quickly you can get both feet hack on the ground after kicking. If there is plenty of room to move about, and you are more agile than your opponent, then by all means try the odd head shot when the opportunity presents itself. Otherwise, restrict your kicks to the opponent's knees or groin.

Extend a kick by sliding on your supporting foot and, wherever possible, replace one-step kicks with the much faster skip-change versions.

8

FOOT SWEEPS AND HOOKS

INTRODUCTION

Foot sweeps and hooks are unbalancing techniques used against the opponent's ankles, shins or lower legs to make him lose his balance. This loss of balance may be complete so the opponent falls to the floor, or partial so he is distracted. Whichever is the case, the opponent is momentarily rendered incapable of responding in a co-ordinated manner to your attack, so an effective technique delivered at that time is almost certain to succeed.

Applying foot sweeps and hooks correctly requires a high level of skill and timing. And it is not enough merely to sweep or hook the opponent – a follow-up in the form of a strike or hold is essential to take him out of the running. Sometimes the follow-up fails because you are surprised when the technique actually works: you hesitate and the opponent has time to recover. Other times the opponent falls unexpectedly and unless you are quick, the opportunity is lost.

PART OF FOOT USED

Use the sole of your foot for sweeping the opponent. Just lift your big toe and turn the others down, as you did for crescent kick in Chapter 7. Then use the big toe side to scoop up the opponent's foot (Fig 157).

Use your instep to hook the opponent's foot, lifting your toes and hooking your instep around the opponent's Achilles' tendon (Fig 158).

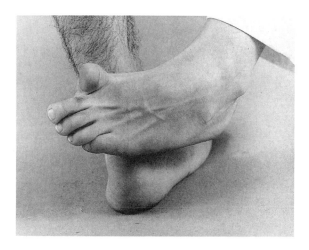

Fig 157 **Use the big toe-side of your foot to scoop the opponent's.**

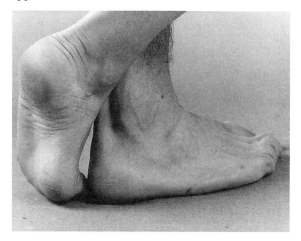

Fig 158 **Hook your instep around the opponent's Achilles tendon.**

TRAINING FOR THE CORRECT FOOT PROFILE

Your partner sits down and extends his right leg. He pulls his left knee up, so the foot is close to his backside. Then he holds an impact pad by its straps, so it protects the outside of his shin and ankle. Take up left fighting stance and throw a high reverse punch with your right fist. Then swing your foot around behind the punch and slam it into the side of the pad, aiming to spin your partner completely around (Fig 159).

The hook needs less effort to apply. Face your partner in fighting stance. Turn until you are both almost facing the same way, hook your instep around his Achilles' tendon and draw his foot forward and up (Fig 160).

PRACTISING THE BASIC SWEEP

The basic sweep uses a fast circular swing of the leg. Begin from fighting stance and twist your shoulders in the same direction as the following sweep. This stretches the muscles in the spine, so they contract more powerfully. Then lift your rear foot from the floor and swing it around and across the front of your body. Form your foot into the correct configuration and skim it over the mat to the target.

Allow your supporting leg to swivel, but don't overdo it. Lean back slightly, maintain an effective guard and keep your face away from the opponent's flailing arms (Fig 161). Use a scooping action both to lift and displace the opponent's foot.

Don't lift your sweep because not only will you lose control of it, but you may also strike the wrong part of the opponent's leg, with consequent loss of effectiveness. Similarly, don't scoop against the side of his knee because though this may cause long-term injury to his knee joint, it is ineffective as a sweeping technique.

HOOKING TECHNIQUES

Perform roundhouse kick with the right foot to the side of the opponent's head. It doesn't matter whether you use a step-up, or a kick off the back

Fig 159 **Slam your foot hard into the pad, aiming to spin your partner around.**

Fig 160 **Use the hook to draw the opponent's foot up and forwards.**

leg; the object is to reach out for the target. The opponent leans back to avoid it, so bring your foot to a stop as soon as you can and drop it to the outside of his leading left foot (Fig 162). Because the opponent is still leaning back from the kick, he isn't bearing down with full weight on his leading foot and it is easier to move.

Retain the hip twist used for your roundhouse kick and hook your instep behind the opponent's Achilles' tendon. Then turn your hips sharply away from the opponent, drawing his trapped foot forward and up. Lift the opponent's leading foot well clear of the ground and draw it forwards, causing him to lose his balance.

Your forward lean in this action has the effect of rendering his flailing arms useless: your face is well out of range, but maintain your guard up as a final defence.

This action is a good example of how a well performed hook clearly draws the opponent's foot in the direction in which it is pointing, and causes an overbalance as a result.

MORE ADVANCED SWEEPING TECHNIQUES

Begin from a left fighting stance and throw a fast reverse punch into the opponent's face. Go for maximum range and allow your hips to turn fully behind the action. Your fist, growing rapidly larger and larger in his visual field will occupy his attention while you set up the next part of the combination.

Provided you are slightly but obviously just out of range, the opponent is most likely to draw back his head from the punch, shifting weight over his rear foot and allowing the leading foot to lighten. Your rear foot then swings around, striking the side of his ankle with the sole. Follow-through with a scooping action to lift the foot.

The effect of this is to jar the opponent's foot to the side. If he still has residual weight on it, he will fall outwards against the direction of the sweeping action. But, if he has only slight weight on his leading foot, then you may succeed only in turning his centre line away from you.

Fig 161 **Keep your face back from the opponent's flailing arms.**

Fig 162 **Drop the spent roundhouse kick to the outside of the opponent's foot.**

Fig 163 **For maximum efficiency, aim to get your scooping foot around the back of the opponent's ankle.**

Fig 164 **Put the opponent on the defensive by throwing a powerful reverse punch at his jaw.**

If you moved forward over your supporting leg as you applied the sweep, then you may find you are close enough to curve the sole of your foot all the way around and into the opponent's Achilles' tendon (Fig 163). In this case, only a light impact will drive his foot in the direction in which it is pointing.

Provided you haven't turned your own body too far, it should be possible to close quickly and strike him before he repositions himself.

Note that the opponent's foot was jarred or knocked to the side. There was no smooth drawing action such as you get with the typical hook.

DOUBLE FOOT SWEEP

Begin from a right fighting stance, while the opponent faces you in left stance. Snap punch into his face with your leading fist, then throw a long-ranging reverse punch in quick succession. Aim the second punch into his face as well, the object being to force the opponent to shift weight on-to his back leg (Fig 164).

Step forward quickly with your left leg, even as you begin to pull back the reverse punch. Turn your toes outwards. Use the pull-back of the reverse punch to help thrust out your right arm so it bars across the front of the opponent's chest (Fig 165). Then swing your right leg into the back of the opponent's. If your advance was powerful enough, then your right hip slams into his left hip as your right foot reaps both his feet. Finish the job by toppling him backwards with the arm bar (Fig 166).

Reverse Foot Sweep

Foot sweeps can also be performed with a reverse action that turns the back of your leg into the opponent's, but as you can imagine, such techniques need a lot of skill. Use this technique when the opponent performs either an orthodox rear leg roundhouse to the face, or the step-up version. In both cases, the opponent turns his centre line away from straight ahead and leans back to counterbalance the weight of his kicking leg. The supporting leg is lifted by the kick with less weight than you might imagine on the supporting foot.

Fig 165 **Step forward and throw your right arm across the opponent's chest.**

Fig 166 **Then bar the opponent backwards over your right knee.**

Slide into the opponent and drop your shoulders while throwing your weight forward to free the rear leg. Move your centre of gravity over your leading leg and spin on the front foot (Fig 167). Sweep your rear leg around in a wide arc, moving in the opposite direction to the opponent's kicking leg. As long as you move forward enough, your calf will strike the back of the opponent's supporting leg as your turning hip jars against him (Fig 168). The combination of these two actions both lifts the opponent and reaps his supporting foot, causing him to roll over your back.

TACTICAL USE OF SWEEPS AND HOOKS

The benefit of applying a foot sweep or hook to a moving or lightened leg cannot be over emphasised. Even a light karateka can sweep a heavier opponent when the latter is in the process of moving his centre of gravity. Sweeping a firmly rooted opponent is another matter entirely and you should never attempt this.

With certain provisos, it is possible to sweep the opponent's foot in any direction, though the way

Fig 167 **Drop under the developing kick.**

Fig 168 **Spin around and reap the supporting leg.**

it is pointing is always the line of least resistance. The skilled karateka uses this fact to gain maximum effect from minimum power. The unskilled karateka simply hacks the opponent's ankles and shins, most likely injuring both of them in the process.

Sweep the opponent's foot as he steps into you. If your timing is right, you will succeed in moving his foot inwards or outwards just as he is putting his weight on to it. If you sweep his advancing foot outwards, he will fall diagonally forwards on to his face. If you take it inwards, he will fall on to his back and shoulder. Be ready to attack without hesitation.

The most powerful leg sweeps use a strong hip action, but beware of over-using it. I have seen such a sweep pass under the targeted foot (the opponent saw the sweep coming and lifted it), spinning the karateka around until his back faced the opponent. So aim at a compromise and don't ever turn your centre line too far away from the opponent.

As I mentioned at the beginning of this chapter, the follow-up is as important as the sweep or hook. Reverse punch is most frequently used, the hips turning towards the opponent and the knees flexing strongly to inject body weight into the impact. The groin is a good target for reverse punch, as is the side of the jaw.

Axe kick is extremely dangerous because the opponent's torso is trapped between your heel and the mat, and so cannot recoil. In such circumstances, impact to the centre of the opponent's chest can cause a heart block: take care.

9

FREESTYLE BLOCKING TECHNIQUES

INTRODUCTION

Blocks are one of the least studied aspects of classical karate training in terms of how well fitted they are for the job they are expected to do. In the interest stakes, they lag far behind attacking techniques and the approach to them simply seems to be, 'Let's get the opponent's technique out the way so I can clobber him!'. As though reflecting this attitude, blocks generally seem to be the least refined part of syllabus.

One type simply smashes the opponent's attack away with brute force. Another uses a primitive form of deflection to meet the opponent's force at an angle. In both cases, however, the emphasis is on blocking the technique. But in this chapter we consider ways of blocking the opponent, so his follow-up techniques are made more difficult.

THE THEORY OF BLOCKING TECHNIQUES

I want first to cover a number of general points about blocking, the first of which is that the block must be made quickly enough to deal with a realistic attack. This rules out those which rely upon the pull-back of the non-blocking arm to generate power for the blocking action. This also rules out circular blocks. Both of the foregoing are no doubt very good for basic training, but they are totally ineffective in a sparring situation.

My first point therefore is, that all blocking actions must use the minimum of movement,

because only then can they be employed quickly enough. If you think about it, this reduces all blocking actions to a short, crisp action in which deflection is achieved not by force, but by skill. Therefore, all the usual mechanisms needed to generate force – pull-back, hip twist, circular movements, double arm swings etc. – are all ruled out.

The second point I want to make is that blocks must not only aim for the minimum movement, but they must also try to achieve maximum deflection of the incoming technique. Novices often fail to achieve this, with the result that a punch aimed at the jaw is swept upwards by a rising block and hits the forehead instead. Similarly, poor mid-section blocks deflect attacks aimed at the solar plexus into the ribs, and ineffective lower blocks sweep the kick into the hip. All these faults are symptoms of insufficient deflection.

Contrast them with the wide sweeps taught in basic blocks, where the attack is deflected well to the side. This is safe, but it is also wasteful, because it then takes longer to retrieve the blocking arm. So deflection must be adequate, but not excessive. The old saying 'A miss is as good as a mile' applies here.

The third point worth mentioning is the specificity of blocks. Many blocks are fairly restricted in their application and when misapplied, the attacking technique is not deflected. Specialised blocks are typically used by skilled karateka who are able correctly to interpret the cues that tell them which attacking technique is on its way.

Fig 169 **Palm of the hand has a small deflection cross section.**

Fig 170 **The forearm has a much larger deflection cross section.**

Often these specialised blocks use only a small part of the body – such as the palm of the hand – to sweep the attack in the correct direction (Fig 169). Now the palm of the hand has a pretty small deflection surface area and if you are inaccurate when using it . . .

Contrast this with forearm blocks. These use the whole length of the forearm, giving a sweep of up to 30 cm in height (Fig 170). Clearly, this provides a much wider margin of error. Double blocks increase this margin still further, though they suffer from the serious disadvantage of tying up both hands. So forearm blocks using just the one arm would seem to be the best compromise for the less skilled karateka.

The fourth point is that the blocking action must be applied correctly to the attacking technique. Blocks are usually active rather than passive – they apply controlled force to deflect the attacker's energy. Contrast this with passive blocking, where a limb is simply left in the path of the attack (Fig 171). Though deflection energies need not be great to achieve an effect, they must nevertheless be applied in the correct manner. Thus, a lower parry must not meet the full force of a front kick (Fig 172). Were this to happen (and it regularly does!), the forearm would probably lose its battle against the shin.

Still on this fourth point, I should mention how the blocking action can be made even more active by rotating the forearm. This both stiffens the arm and adds an extra sharpness to the blocking impact. In some cases, it also facilitates the block in other ways, but I shall show this later on by reference to particular techniques.

The fifth point about blocks is that they should not be aimed solely at the attacking technique itself. I have never seen this point mentioned in any martial arts manual or syllabus, though it is an obvious one if you think about it. Thus, an incoming punch is met with a forearm block and swept to the side (see again Fig 170). So what? If you have blocked on the wrong side, you have merely turned the opponent's upper body and encouraged him to use his other fist. And even if you block him on his closed side, he is still able to withdraw and counter-attack.

You must therefore block into him – crossing his techniques as you do so. Your block must always travel outwards from your body and towards the centre line of the opponent (Fig 173). Never block with a sweep that travels simply from low to high, or from side to side. All truly effective blocking actions travel diagonally.

There is a second benefit to doing this. The incoming technique requires time to develop full power, and going out to meet it means deflecting it before full power is on tap. Furthermore, blocking well out from your body gives you a margin of error in which to do something if the block should fail. Pity the poor karateka who has blocked close to the body, for if this fails . . .

Fig 173 **Your block always travels into the opponent's centre line.**

Fig 171 **Passive blocking simply interposes a limb between the technique and its target.**

Fig 172 **The block must not meet the incoming technique in head-on collision!**

I want to enter a caveat here. When going into the opponent, keep your chin out of the way! Many people lead with their faces as they close with the attacker. Keep your back near to vertical, though a slight forward lean is permissible. Relax your shoulders but let them curve forward and, above all keep control of your arms. Novices concentrate on the blocking action and ignore what the other hand is doing. You should move both arms together and be economical with their action, never moving either more than is necessary.

The sixth point is about always keeping your body turned so your centre line faces the opponent. This is critical! Each time you block, go into him, projecting your blocking energy through your own centre line. Do not do as so many schools do, and turn your body away from the attack (Fig 174). This may cause the attack to miss, but it also ensures that you are powerless to make an immediate and effective response.

In many of the scooping blocks, for example, you are obliged, having twisted away and blocked, to twist back before you can use a power-

Fig 174 **Never turn your own centre line away from the opponent as you block.**

Fig 175 **The opponent's punch is deflected by your right forearm.**

Fig 176 **Then your block carries on and becomes a counter attacking punch into the opponent's face.**

ful strike. This violates the first rule of blocking in that you have added an unnecessary and time-consuming action. It is true that you could lash out with a back fist, but you will find that whenever your centre line faces away from the opponent, the power your strike generates is limited.

The seventh point concerns the position of your hands as you block, and it begins where I left off earlier. Block in such a manner that at least one of your hands is near the target. Only then can a counter-attack be applied quickly enough. Beware blocking the opponent and then having to retrieve your non-blocking arm from the hip. Instead, bring both fists close to the opponent so you can strike him quickly with either. The most advanced blocks combine deflection with a counter-attack so the opponent's punch is first deflected, then the deflecting fist carries on into the opponent's face (Figs 175 & 176). Such techniques, however, require a formidable level of skill.

The eighth point reiterates and adds to one we looked at a moment ago. Do not let your block cross your own centre line (Fig 177). Not only is this unnecessary, but it also makes the technique weak. Keep each hand to the correct side of the body and you will be able to use it directly. Lose control of your hands so they cross the centre line willy-nilly and you will lose vital time retrieving them before you can apply a powerful technique. 'But,' I hear you argue, 'if my block doesn't cross the centre line, then the incoming technique will not be swept far enough to the side and it will still hit me!' This would be true were it not for the fact that body evasion must be used to set you up in the correct position for any block.

Don't just flail your arms about and expect them to stop a determined attack, because a block response does not just entail moving your arms – you must position your body too. Re-read the paragraphs on centre line and combine your block with an angled advance into the opponent.

My ninth point concerns the application of power during the blocking action. Typically, novices 'focus' their blocks and go for maximum power at the end of the movement. But what happens if the attack is faster than anticipated? Supposing a kick catches your lower parry before the latter has taken up its final position? The novice's

arm is moving fast, but it lacks energy, so the block fails and injury is likely.

Trying to block with a rigid arm does not work either, because taut muscles cause a loss of speed. The answer is to use whole-body energy and to move into the attack. Stepping back is not a valid response because a skilled opponent will then simply move forward and force you further onto the defensive. And never fully straighten your elbow during a block since this robs it of its resilience and power.

Aim to make the block effective throughout its range of movement, so even if you are caught unprepared, you aren't left defenceless. You must be well guarded at all times. Remember – your block must be effective regardless of the circumstances in which it is used. A block must not only work effectively in the training hall – it should also work in the cinema, or on the street!

Fig 177 **Never let your hands cross your own centre line.**

APPLYING THEORY TO FREESTYLE BLOCKS

Rising Block

There are two types of rising block, the first of which is the upwards rolling block. As its name implies, this version uses a rising and rolling action of the blocking forearm to deflect the opponent's punch upwards, or diagonally upwards and to the side. The forearm rotates as it rises, so the little finger edge finishes uppermost. Make sure that the degree of deflection is adequate, so the punch clears the intended target and the blocking forearm does not obscure the eyes.

The skilled user turns his body so the centre line is directed towards the opponent. The blocking forearm rises and rotates in the normal manner, but a shrugging action of the shoulders takes it forwards as well as up, changing it into an upwards *diagonal* movement that closes with the attacking technique. Sometimes this means that the block is applied high on the opponent's arm, though this need not always be the case (Fig 178).

Do not lean forward as you apply the block. This is a common and dangerous fault, because it brings your face too close to the opponent. Use only the power of your shoulder muscles and the springiness of your elbow to make the block effective. Don't lock up the rest of your body or you will slow your follow-up. If you find yourself too far away to block correctly, then simply use a short forward slide to close distance and, if necessary, adjust your angle by means of a turning motion of the body.

Apply the block so as to close the opponent off, stopping him from using his other arm by following up with a hooking forearm block. This forces

Fig 178 **Block high on the opponent's arm.**

Fig 179 **Force the opponent's arm across his own body and counter attack.**

Fig 180   Your blocking forearm rises and rotates until the little finger turns upwards.

Fig 181   Use line to your advantage and block to his closed side.

the opponent's trapped arm across his upper body and obscures his counter attack (Fig 179).

Use this version of rising block to counter-attacks to the face and body.

The second version of rising block is effective only against attacks to the face. It uses a longer action to take the blocking forearm diagonally upwards and forwards.

Begin from a fighting stance, sliding forward on the front foot and thrusting the forward guard hand into the centre line of your body. The fist rises above your head and the forearm rotates so the muscular part of the forearm turns to face upwards (Fig 180). This makes the elbow joint more resilient and saves the bones of the forearm from injury.

Your wrist and forearm meet the opponent's wrist at an early stage in the development of his technique and deflects it to the side. This deflection is most obviously seen when the opponent swings a hammer-fist down on to the top of your head. His forearm meets yours at an angle and, like rainwater running down a sloping roof, it is diverted to the side.

Fig 182   Continue the block on so it becomes a punch.

129

By using line to your advantage, you can block to his closed side, and if you block to his open side (Fig 181), then simply hook your fist around and punch him in the side of his jaw (Fig 182).

Make the block more effective by going to meet the opponent, and by reaching for his technique with your blocking arm. Be sure to guard your chin by keeping the non-blocking fist close to it.

I have not described x-block, because this ties up both arms and leaves you defenceless.

Inner And Outer Forearm Blocks

The next two blocks to consider are the inner and outer forearm blocks. The same block is described in at least two different ways by different schools, so to avoid confusion, we shall describe them here as follows:

1   when the arms hang naturally by the sides, the thumb side of the fist turns

inwards towards the thighs. Therefore the thumb side of the forearm is the 'inner' forearm.

2   the little finger side of the arm faces outwards, so that part of the forearm is the outer part.

The first to be considered is the inner forearm block. This uses a rotational forearm action, coupled with a windscreen-wiper action of the shoulder joint to swing the forearm up and into the opponent's punching arm. The elbow is bent so the blocking hand – usually a fist – is level with the top of your shoulder. It is very dangerous to straighten the arm too much, since this makes the block very weak indeed. This is why the novice is always taught to keep his elbow close to the ribs.

The basic block uses pull-back of the non-blocking arm to power the deflection, but as I mentioned earlier, this wastes too much time and

Fig 183   **The blocking action begins with the thumb vertical.**

Fig 184   **Then the forearm rotates so the palm turns upwards.**

renders the block ineffective for actual sparring. However, the block tends to be weak without this pull-back, so other means to strengthen it must be found.

The first is to turn into the direction of the block as it is being applied. This generates power from the hip. The second is to thrust both shoulders forward in a shrugging action similar to that used in the head block described above. The forearm travels diagonally forward and across the body (though it never crosses the centre line!) with the thumb uppermost (Fig 183). Then the hip engages and the hand rotates to a palm-upwards position (Fig 184). Therefore it no longer simply strikes the attacking limb; instead it travels forward and into the opponent, so the block takes place almost as an afterthought, as it were. This sometimes means that the opponent is blocked higher up his arm than you might have expected (Fig 185).

Step forward if you need to close distance, but never lean forward since this advances the chin. As long as you thrust hard enough forwards with the block, then it is not even necessary to rotate the hand fully palm-upwards and satisfactory blocks can be made even with the thumb upwards and the hand only partially rotated. Remember – do not block against the attack – block forward and into it! The correctly applied inner forearm block does not simply deflect a technique; it opens the opponent to your counter-attack.

Remember to leave the elbow slightly bent. A straight arm is weak and vulnerable, whereas a slightly flexed elbow is resilient and powerful. Strengthen the elbow by clenching the fingers and stiffening the wrist slightly, and above all, do not allow your elbow to swing outwards since this severely weakens the blocking action.

Novices practise outer forearm block with a chopping action that uses the little finger edge of the hand and side of the wrist/forearm to knock an attack to the side. The blocking action is enhanced both by hip twist and through a long circular action that sweeps the forearm across the body. Ignore the idea of pulling back the non-blocking arm even in elementary practice, since this is both slow and wasteful of effort.

The advanced block uses much the same abbreviated action, except that it changes from chopping to thrusting hand. The thrust is direct, so it

Fig 185 **Thrust your block forwards as you apply it, taking the opponent on his upper arm.**

wastes less time and is quicker. But for all that, it is no less powerful. Impact is on the forearm and back of wrist, with the palm turned upwards.

Take up stance and turn your hips slightly away from the direction in which you will block. Extend the fingers of your right hand, turning the hand palm-downwards and draw your leading guard hand closer to your body (Fig 186). Twist your hips to face the opponent fully and as the shoulders are twisting to their new position, the right elbow moves into the ribs. Begin rotating the right hand even as it moves – don't leave the final twist until the last moment (Fig 187) The right hand then thrusts out and the elbow straightens as the shoulders take up their final position. Tighten the muscles of the forearm and wrist sharply as the palm turns upwards (Fig 188).

The kinetics of outside block are very important. There must be a slight delay between the hips turning and the shoulders following, to make use of the twisting tension in the spinal muscles. Also allow a further slight delay between the shoulders turning into their final position and extension of

131

Fig 186 **Begin with your hips turned away from the opponent and your right arm extended.**

Fig 187 **Turn your hips to the front and draw your right hand inwards.**

Fig 188 **Thrust the blocking arm out and rotate it so the palm turns upwards.**

the blocking arm to help make the final thrusting action stronger. Finally, shrug your shoulders forward and lead with the blocking shoulder.

Each part of the movement must flow smoothly into the next at just the right time. Avoid jerkiness and accelerate smoothly all the way to the final position. Don't forget to bring your blocking elbow close to your ribs before thrusting it out. By these means, the block becomes a thrust into the opponent's body which, on the way, encounters and deflects his punch.

Hooking Block

A third type of forearm block is hooking block. This uses neither the inside nor the outside of the forearm, but its lower surface.

Hooking block is quite a strong technique when it is thrust forwards and into the opponent with a palm-downwards hand position. This allows the lower forearm to glance over the top of the attacking technique before travelling on into the opponent's face.

As with outer block, the kinetics of hooking block are all-important. Deliver it with a twisting motion of the hips that turns the blocking side towards the opponent. Follow this with a shrugging action of the shoulders, thrusting your blocking arm forward into the opponent's punch or grab. Step forward to close distance, barring the opponent's blocked arm across his own body (Fig 189). This will make it impossible for him to push your arm away because he is pushing against your body – not just against your arm. Also, the block concludes with your elbow very near to his forearm, so he is obliged to apply pressure close to the fulcrum, and this is more difficult than just pushing away your forearm.

From the final position you can follow on for a direct attack into your opponent's jaw by using the blocking hand (Fig 190). However, don't release his arm by first withdrawing your block – instead, go straight for the target with either a short, jolting palm heel or a straight punch.

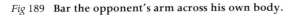

Fig 189 **Bar the opponent's arm across his own body.**

Fig 190 **Take the blocking arm direct into the opponent's jaw.**

Knife Block

Knife block uses the little finger edge of the open hand to deflect the opponent's wrist or forearm. Though popular in the basic techniques of classical karate, it is not often used as such in freestyle. Use it as a short thrusting strike with the edge of the leading guard hand that deflects the opponent's forearm (Fig 191). Then carry it forward as a palm-heel strike into his jaw.

Also use it as you step back from the opponent's advance, drawing back your leading guard hand and thrusting forward with the rear hand (Figs 192 & 193).

Knife block also works as a fail-safe move, when your centre line has been turned. Imagine you have thrown an unsuccessful roundhouse kick and landed in a sideways-facing position. Quickly turn your hips back, allowing the shoulders to follow and cut across your body with both hands

(Figs 194 & 195). Complete the sequence with either a reverse punch or a palm-heel strike delivered with the blocking hand.

Palm-heel Block

The palm of the hand makes an effective, fast slapping block which can be used either horizontally or vertically. It smacks the incoming technique off course, sometimes striking near the wrist/ankle, where great leverage is not necessary. Use this block from a distance – after you have stepped back – then close range immediately with a front kick counter-attack (Fig 196).

Cup your hand slightly, so the fingers curl forwards. This stiffens the forearm and makes the wrist resilient. The fingers remain straight and tight together while the thumb curls around to reinforce the palm.

Palm-heel block can also be used like hooking

Fig 191 **Thrust knife hand block forward and into the opponent's arm.**

Fig 192 **Step back and thrust forward your rear guarding hand.**

Fig 193 **Draw back the extended hand and use this action to power the knife block.**

Fig 194 **Take both arms out behind you . . .**

Fig 195 . . . then swing them both together across your body.

block, in the form of a strong thrust into the opponent. This causes the block to strike higher up the opponent's arm, closing his body off and preventing a fast follow-up. Power for the advanced block comes from a twisting motion of the hips with a shrugging action of the shoulders. The blocking shoulder leads, though the face should not be brought forward (Fig 197).

Lower Parry

Lower parry uses a powerful downwards arc to sweep a wide area free from attacking techniques, but even at full extension, the elbow of the blocking forearm is never fully straightened. It is always slightly bent so the elbow is resilient. This resilience also comes from a strong hand position in which the fingers are clenched and the wrist bent.

The novice is taught to move well away from the attack, using both arms together in a combination outer block/lower parry. This sweeps a very wide area indeed and is excellent for making safe. However, the advanced student will not merely want to make safe – he will want to carry the fight to the opponent. With this in mind, advanced lower parry is applied with more of a thrust than a swing.

The advanced block requires you to move diagonally forward so the kick misses by the smallest possible amount. Indeed, less emphasis is placed upon making safe and more reliance is placed upon the block. However, since you have moved only so far as is barely necessary, you are left close enough to push the opponent completely off balance with a combination of lower parry and palm-heel (Fig 198).

In classical schools, one version of lower parry is made with the body's centre line rotating away from the direction of the block. Though this may be effective at deflecting the attack, you then have to twist back in order to counter-attack.

Fig 196 **Use palm-heel block from a distance, then counter with front kick.**

Fig 197 **Palm heel-block can also be used from a shorter range to close the opponent off.**

Fig 198 **Use lower parry to deflect the kick and push the opponent off balance with a simultaneous palm-heel strike.**

Scooping Block

Scooping block curls the cupped hand under the opponent's kick, lifting it up and forward. Now some schools of karate twist the body as the block is applied, so the centre line is turned away from the attacker. Certainly this may prove effective at deflecting the kick, but it also leaves the defender in a very weak position. It is much better to withdraw directly from the kick, by rocking back into a short cat stance while curling your blocking hand under the advancing foot (Fig 199). Lift the trapped foot and take it to his closed side, so the opponent's centre line is turned and his opportunities for immediate counter-attack are reduced to a wild swinging of his arms.

Double Blocks

As I mentioned at the beginning of the chapter, double blocks are unspecialised and sweep a wide area clear of incoming techniques. Though these tend not to be used so much by the skilled karateka, they are very useful to the novice and intermediate stage student. With this in mind I will describe two of the most effective double blocks. Note that both use crisp, direct and minimal arm movement to provide a good cover.

Begin from a high right fighting stance and twist your hips strongly to the left, so you virtually turn about-face. As you are turning, drive your right hand down into a low rising block and thrust the left out into an inner forearm block. Both arm actions go on at the same time and both finish together – exactly as the hip action comes to a dead stop (Fig 200).

Reread the paragraphs on each block and ensure you do them correctly and without bias to either one. Your left forearm sweeps the upper body and face clear, while the low rising block clears the lower body. Note that the elbows of both arms are fairly close together and an equal distance from your body, so there is no gap in the cover provided. Both blocks thrust forwards to meet the attacking technique, but neither hand crosses the centre line.

Fig 200   **Thrust your right hand down into a low rising block and the left into an inner forearm block.**

Fig 201   **Thrust the left arm downwards in a lower parry and drive out the right as an outer forearm block.**

The second block uses a combination of lower parry and outer forearm block. Again, begin from right fighting stance and swivel your hips sharply to the left, so you turn about-face. Use this action to power a downwards thrust with the left arm and an outwards thrust with the right (Fig 201). Perform both blocks simultaneously and go to meet the attack. This version also provides good cover from lower body to face.

TACTICAL BLOCKING

Don't waste your time trying to block fast, short snap punches to the face. Just turn your upper body slightly, so your chin drops into your shoulder and your guard hand moves across their path. Very fast attacking punches can be taken on the shoulders and arms, but do not drop your guard even for an instant.

Never stand still, or your blocking capability will be swamped. Instead, keep on the move, constantly changing your range and adjusting your line so the opponent has nothing to zero-in on.

Blocks come into their own when you are dealing with kicks or attempts to grab hold of you. These move more slowly than snap punches, so there is time to set up a proper blocking action. But always make safe by combining your block with an evasion.

10

COMBINATION TECHNIQUES

INTRODUCTION

Combination techniques are series of basic techniques linked together in some sort of logical order. In classical schools, combinations are taught in class lines with students flailing at the air. The freestyle karateka, however, will practise them against a punch-bag or target mitts, because only then will he learn accuracy, timing and control over distance and line.

In this chapter I will not be setting down lists of combination techniques for you to try. Instead I will describe what makes a good combination and, once you understand this, you will be able to develop your own.

THE THEORY OF COMBINATION TECHNIQUES

Playing snooker is not just a matter of getting the ball into the pocket, it's also about positioning the cue ball to make the next pot. So it is with combination techniques. The opening technique, be it punch, strike or kick, hits the target and coincidentally sets up the next technique – so that also hits the target. It can set up the next technique in two ways: first it can create an opening where one didn't exist before and secondly, it sets up your body in such a way that the following technique is facilitated. We'll look at both these aspects later in the chapter.

If you are a large and strong person, then only one or two sledgehammer blows may be enough to demolish the opponent. But if you are a lightweight taking on a much larger person, then a whole rain of blows may be necessary to achieve the same result.

You may be facing a good defensive fighter – everything you throw at him, he takes out with his defensive screen of blocks and evasions. In this case, you can either force him to switch on to the offensive, or you can subject him to such a pressure of attack that just one slip is all that is needed for your technique to get through. And once he's hurt, the next technique may find it a bit easier to reach the target. Martial art historians will recognise this tactic from certain classic swordfighting traditions.

So let's look at some of the ingredients of successful combination techniques. The first is the obvious one, that successive techniques must arrive on the target within an instant of each other. Unless two punches arrive in a short interval, the opponent will see and deal with them as two separate techniques. You might throw a snap punch at the opponent's face, meaning to punch him on the nose. If this is the case, then your punch will be correctly ranged, fast and potentially dangerous. The opponent sees this fist growing larger in his field of vision (Fig 202) and decides to do something about it.

However, disguised by your fist is a short step up of the rear leg, so you can lift off with a roundhouse kick to the opponent's jaw. But, if you delay the kick, the opponent will recover from the punch, see the kick and take the appropriate counter-measures. So there's the first rule of good

Fig 202 **The opponent sees your fist growing larger in his field of vision.**

combination technique: one technique must follow the next quickly.

It is easier to fire a fast volley of punches because each is moving only a short distance. It is not so easy to launch kicks in quick succession because the legs just don't work that quickly.

The second rule is that of target separation. By this I mean aim the first technique at the face and the second at the opponent's mid section. This forces him to switch attention between high and low incoming attacks, and this can swamp his defence screen.

The third rule is to mix linear and circular techniques. A straight punch to the face produces the best window of opportunity because your fist closes off his vision and a following roundhouse kick coming in from the side may then approach unnoticed. Though fast linear attacks straight into the opponent's face make the best feints, slower moving circular attacks to the side of his head may not even be seen. Combine the second and third rules so you use a mixture of circular and linear techniques to widely separated targets.

The fourth rule is to use one technique to set up the next – think about an analogy with snooker. Stand in left fighting stance and throw a powerful reverse punch into the opponent's face. Really reach out and try to hit him on the nose. You will find that your punch takes weight off your trailing leg and your right hip may turn so far forward behind the punching action that the heel rises from the mat. This is quite a normal reaction, so use it to launch a mid-section roundhouse kick into the opponent's floating ribs. Your weight is already off the back leg and your hips are set up perfectly for the roundhouse kick. This means that the kick can be delivered pretty quickly after the punch.

Observant readers will have noted that the above example combines all the rules for good combination technique so far discussed – a linear strike to the opponent's face to distract him, followed by a widely separated circular attack to the floating ribs.

The fifth rule is that only meaningful techniques can be used in combination with each other. Imagine trying to distract the opponent with a snap punch so as to create a window of opportunity for your more powerful reverse punch. This will fail if your snap punch is weak, or is obviously short of the target – the opponent will simply ignore it and concentrate instead upon your reverse punch.

The sixth rule concerns technique/range selections. When you throw your opening technique, the opponent will do one of five things. First, he may not move at all, in which case your technique hits him. Secondly, he may step into your opening technique. This is not likely to happen if you use an effective linear technique. Thirdly, he may step back from your opener, increasing the distance between the two of you. Fourthly, he may step to the side, and fifthly, he may step either diagonally forwards or diagonally backwards.

In the second case, engagement distance closes sharply. If your opener was a snap punch, then do not be tempted to kick or you will be caught standing on one leg as he comes barrelling in with fists flying. Follow your snap punch with other punches and strikes while moving to a diagonal and turning your centre line towards him.

In the third instance, engagement distance

opens out and a kick is in order. After your snap punch, follow up with a skipping front kick. This reaches further than a punch and may reach him, even though he is out of hand technique range.

If he steps to the side, then engagement distance will remain the same and what suited you for an opener will suit you for a follow-up. Throw your snap punch, then follow with reverse punches. However, in order to maintain a fast and balanced delivery, keep your centre line turned towards him.

If he steps diagonally forward, then range will shorten and a kick would be totally inappropriate – especially if he has moved to your closed side. Turn to face him, shorten your stance and fire off a volley of punches. If he steps back diagonally, either step forwards with further hand techniques, or use a kick followed by hand techniques.

The opponent who backpedals from your attacks should be run down by either a fast forward advance while using hand techniques, or you should overtake him with a combination of kicks. Throw a long-reaching right roundhouse kick to his head, going all out for full range. Drop the spent foot in a forward position (but watch out for foot sweep!), with your hips turned sideways-on (Fig 203). Bring your weight forward and turn your hips at the same time, so your back presents to the opponent (Fig 204). Then pick up your left foot and thrust it backwards and into his midsection or groin (Fig 205).

Note how the roundhouse kick sets up the straight back kick. This is important because it means a fast sequence. You couldn't do this, for example, if you tried to follow the roundhouse with a right foot side kick, because it would mean

Fig 203 **Drop the spent kick in a forwards position with the hips turned away from the opponent.**

Fig 204 **Turn your back on the opponent but look over your shoulder.**

Fig 205 **Thrust your kick out with the heel leading.**

having to stop first and then reverse the natural action of your hips.

One of the key features of good combination techniques is to be able to use an effective technique from whichever position you find yourself in. In practice this means having no weak sides. If you find your left side techniques are not so accurate or powerful, then devote extra training time to them. A person who can only use one side of his body is 50 per cent less effective than he ought to be.

Let's see how you can use a combination technique to get you out of serious trouble. Perhaps you have swung really hard at the opponent's leading foot with your right, in an attempt to sweep him. Unfortunately, he sees the sweep coming and lifts his foot, so yours just skims under it (Fig 206). You put a lot of effort into the sweep, so it is impossible to stop before your back is fully turned. The answer is not to stop it! Carry on turning, drop your spent right foot to the mat and perform a short-range back kick to the opponent's mid section. Alternatively, drop the right foot as before, then continue rotating and use your left leg to reap both the opponent's with a reverse sweep (Fig 207).

I want to finish this section with a caution: never rely overly much on one combination! The alert opponent will soon begin to notice if you show a preference for linking certain techniques together. So ring the changes from time to time and you won't become a casualty of your own combination technique. Make that your seventh and final rule – don't be predictable!

PRACTISING COMBINATION TECHNIQUE

The object of combination technique training is to be able to throw a combination of punches, a com-

Fig 206 **Your intended sweep passes harmlessly beneath the opponent's raised foot.**

Fig 207 **Continue turning, drop down and reap the opponent's supporting leg.**

bination of kicks, or a combination of both kicks and punches, while advancing, retreating, moving to the side, or simply while more or less standing still. Begin by firing volleys of punches into a suspended bag, aiming for wide separation and mixing hooks with jabs. Duck and weave as you do so. Then begin moving around the bag, hitting as you go. Change to a pair of target mitts, aiming now for speed. Your partner moves them independently in figures-of-eight, even as he himself is moving about. This teaches you how to range on moving targets as you yourself move.

Use a large pad for leg combinations, getting your partner to retreat as you throw a succession of kicks. Try to hit hard with each kick and remedy areas of weakness by extra and specific training. Use skip and step kicking to ensure you are always in range. Try not to get caught with one foot off the ground if he pushes forward unless, that is, you intend to check his advance with a front kick. Otherwise, avoid his onrushes by stepping diagonally and be ready to close the instant he steps back.

You may notice that you tend to connect certain techniques together in a particular way – for example, you may always follow a reverse punch to mid-section with a roundhouse kick to the head. Be on the look-out for this and try to work out alternative combinations that also work for you.

You may feel good with a certain combination, yet it never seems to succeed. In this case, what feels good is simply not working, and you have to be prepared to analyse what is going wrong. Use a partner and/or a mirror to discover what is amiss. You may find that you are tending to use an otherwise good sequence in inappropriate circumstances.

Some people can perform a combination technique like roundhouse kick/reverse punch when moving forward, but they experience all kinds of difficulties when trying it as they retreat. This indicates a lack of versatility which can be remedied by regular practice with a mirror to check that your techniques are well executed. Always aim to beat your reflection to the drop.

11

THROWS, HOLD-DOWNS AND LOCKS IN FREESTYLE KARATE

INTRODUCTION

Only one style of classical karate teaches a wrist hold, and none teach throws or hold-downs as part of the syllabus. Yet you may wish to restrain someone without causing them or yourself injury. The opponent may close inside impact technique range, leaving you trying to out-grapple him. One or both of you may fall to the floor, in which case you need to know how to handle yourself in a prone position.

This chapter deals with the throws, restraint holds and joint locks of freestyle karate. The selection of techniques shown is far from exhaustive and should be thought of as the minimum necessary for developing an overall competence.

All selected techniques satisfy three criteria

1   They are effective over a wide range of different-sized people.
2   They need only the minimum of skill to produce a worthwhile result.
3   They are responses to realistic forms of attack.

Any techniques added by individual freestyle coaches should also conform to these three criteria.

EFFECTIVE THROWING TECHNIQUES

Before beginning practice, you need to learn how to breakfall and, for safety's sake, practise all breakfalls and throws on a properly matted surface.

Back Breakfall

Lie flat on your back and bend your knees slightly, with the soles of your feet pressing against the mat. Lift your head and look at your belt. The head must always be held in this way, because only then will it escape injury from hard contact with the floor. Tap the mat with the whole length of your arms, right down to the palms of your hands.

Then sit up with your legs thrown out and roll backwards, slapping the mat hard with both hands. Do this several times and try to time the slapping action so it is neither too early nor too late. As soon as you have mastered this, go to the next stage in the progression by adopting a squatting position with your arms outstretched in front of you (Fig 208). Then roll on to your back and slap with both arms [Fig 209]. Vary the angle of your arms to your body 30° to 60°, depending on the width of your shoulders, matching the wider separation with a heavier upper body.

Complete the progression by falling back from a standing position, dropping first into a squat before you roll back and slap.

Side Breakfall

Begin practice from a sitting position, with your legs thrown out in front of you. Roll to your right side and slap the mat with your right arm. Try this five times, then repeat the exercise to the left, this time tapping with your left arm. Take up a squatting position with your right foot slightly forward

Fig 208 **Squat down and extend your arms.**

Fig 209 **Roll back and slap with both arms.**

of the left. Then roll to the right five times, slapping down with your right arm as you land. Repeat the exercise to the left.

Take up a standing position and swing your right foot in front of the left, so you overbalance to the right (Fig 210). Slap hard with your right arm (Fig 211). Begin with a bent left leg, so you only gradually increase height as your skill improves. Learn to slap with the whole of your arm, the hand striking the mat at the same time as your body.

Forward Breakfall

Take up a squatting position with your arms extended in front of you. Launch yourself forward, as though to dive on to the mat, but interrupt your flight with the palms of both hands. Let your elbows give under your bodyweight so they soak up the energy of your movement. Then take up a standing position with knees well bent and fall forward on to your face. Reach out with both hands and allow the elbows to bend with a

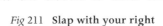

Fig 210 **Swing your right foot across and in front of your left so you overbalance.**

Fig 211 **Slap with your right hand as you land.**

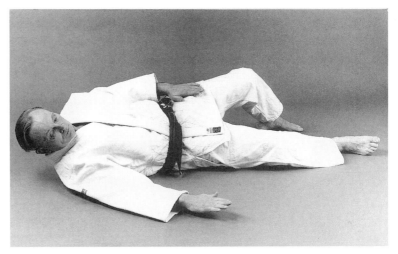

springy action as the palms touch the mat. When you are more confident, practise front breakfall from a fully-upright stance.

Forward Roll-Out

Put your right foot well forward and drop your palm to the mat near to it (Fig 212), so your right knee is outside of the slightly bent right elbow. Don't drop your head between your arms! Straighten your right leg and kick up with the left, so you roll forward over the right elbow and shoulder (Fig 213). These form a natural curve along which the body rolls (Fig 214). Slap down hard with the left arm as the roll-out completes (Fig 215).

Avoid turning your hips to the right because this causes the full weight of the body to land on the hip, producing an inefficient action. Land with your right leg fully extended and the left leg flexed beneath it.

If you go into the fall at speed, the momentum achieved, aided by the slap, can return you to a standing position. To do this, however, you must keep your body in one straight line. Your natural tendency will be to hinge the body as you try to lurch up, but this produces a clumsy roll-out.

Practise on both sides, but don't try rolling breakfall to the left until you have mastered the fall to the right.

The Leg Throw

Take your partner's left lapel in your right hand and grip the sleeve of his right, just above the elbow. Sink your weight by bending your knees slightly and take a half-step forward and outwards with your left leg. Some people prefer to advance the right leg, while others use the classical position and stand with their feet at shoulder's width apart and neither leading the other. Hold your body erect and do not allow the shoulders to hunch up. This is the basic position from which all throws begin (Fig 216).

Draw your partner towards you, so he is forced to take a step. He will put most of his bodyweight on to the leading foot, dragging the other quickly up behind it to re-establish his stance. Never allow your legs to cross your own centre line, or you will immediately become unstable.

When you are both reasonably comfortable at closing and taking hold of each other, move on to practising the throw.

Begin by stepping back a short distance with

Fig 212 **Drop your palm to the floor.**

Fig 213 **Kick up with your left leg.**

your left leg and turn your foot outwards. Pull gently on the opponent's right sleeve with your left arm as you do this. If you do this smoothly, the opponent will tend to step forward with his right leg in order to maintain distance (Fig 217). Don't jerk the opponent or pull sharply on his arm, because his instinctive reaction will be to pull back against you.

The importance of this 'fitting' movement must be emphasised because it is essential for performing the throw correctly.

Lean well forwards, twist your hips and draw the opponent's right arm outwards and to your left. Even as you perform this action, your right hand is pushing and lifting the opponent, so his centre of gravity is taken diagonally backwards. Bring your right foot forward and hook it back into the opponent's leading right leg, so the rear of your knee contacts the rear of his (Fig 218). The opponent will normally release your sleeve in order to breakfall with his left arm, and you let go of his lapel with your right.

Holding on to his sleeve prevents him from rolling away from you and it is then an easy matter to sink your weight by bending your knees. Use this action to add power to a strike or punch.

If you are doing the technique correctly, the throwing action will be short, sharp and effective. If it isn't, then you may not be:

1   Performing the fitting movement correctly;
2   Twisting your hips to help draw the opponent off-balance (this is the most usual fault);
3   Pulling his right arm at the same time as you lift and pull his left shoulder.

It is unnecessary to hook back strongly with your reaping leg. The mechanism of the throw is such that a gentle sweep is all that is required – the opponent is already unbalanced.

Make sure you throw your head and shoulders forward as you apply the technique or your opponent may be able to turn the tables on you and throw you instead.

Quite an effective version of leg throw is one in which you duck under the opponent's hook. Straighten up and execute the throw as before, except that you trap his punching arm by pressing your palm against his shoulder (Fig 219).

As with all subsequent throws, locks and holds, you must practise the technique on both sides, paying particular attention to the weaker side.

Fig 214   **Roll forward over your shoulder.**

Fig 215   **Breakfall with your left hand.**

Fig 216　Take the opponent's lapel in your right hand and his sleeve in your left.

Fig 217　Draw the opponent forward.

Fig 218　Draw the opponent's right sleeve to the side and hook back with your right leg.

Fig 219　Trap the opponent's right arm with your left palm and throw him as before.

Floating Hip Throw

Take up the opening posture again and pull firmly, but not jerkily, with your right hand to make the opponent step a fraction forward with his left leg. Put your left foot directly in front of his, so the big toes are nearly touching (Fig 220). Then let go of his lapel, slipping your right arm under his armpit and around his back at waist height.

Pivot to the left on the toes of your left foot, until your right hip is underneath the opponent's belt. Bend your knees to achieve the correct height. Draw your right foot around as well, so both feet finish up less than shoulder's-width apart. Hold the opponent tightly against your hip by means of your encircling right arm (Fig 221).

Straighten your knees as you twist your shoulders and head to the left, drawing his sleeve across with your left arm.

The result of this is first to lift, then to tilt the opponent over your right hip, so he falls on to his back in front of you (Fig 222). Release your hold around his waist once you feel he is going over and this will allow him to breakfall properly. But keep hold of his right sleeve, so he cannot roll away from your follow-up technique.

Let's now examine the throw in greater detail.

The first point is that both your feet must be inside the opponent's – never to the outside of them. The latter is a very common fault of novices. Should you happen to place your right foot too far to the right, then you will find that you have lost much of the lifting power of your hips and even if you succeed in lifting the opponent, your balance will become precarious as you attempt to throw him.

The second point is that you must lift the opponent by the straightening action of your knees – not by leaning your upper body and trying to drag him over it. Your leg muscles are extremely powerful and even a light person can lift a heavy

Fig 220 **Put your left foot in front of the opponent's.**

Fig 221 **Hold the opponent to you with your encircling right arm.**

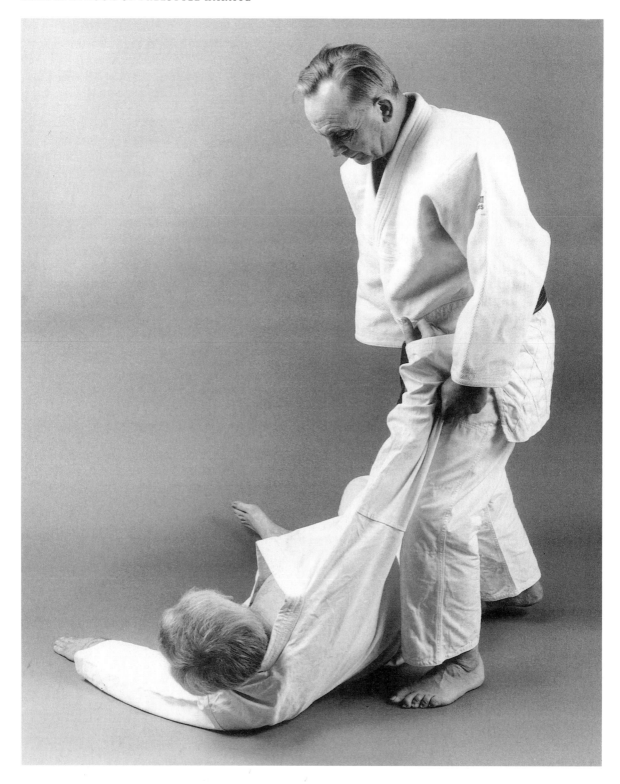

Fig 222   The opponent is lifted and drawn over your hip, falling to the mat in front of you.

one when the knees are fully straightened from a partially bent position. Having said that, do not bend the knees too much, since this makes them susceptible to injury.

Once you have understood the basics of the throw, perform ten practice throws to the stage where the opponent has just been lifted from the ground. When you are happy with this, perform the throw ten times all the way through

Neck Throw

Begin from the now-familiar opening stance and draw the opponent smoothly towards you, relying more on your lapel grasp than on the sleeve hold. Step back a half-pace with your right foot as you draw him forward. The object is to encourage him to step forward with his left foot.

Then turn your body and take a diagonal back step with your leading left foot, so it comes to lie

facing outwards behind the right. Switch your main efforts to the sleeve hold and draw the opponent strongly towards you by his right arm. He will be forced to step forwards in order to take all the weight off his right foot (Fig 223).

Let go of your lapel hold and throw your right hand around the opponent's neck. At the same time, turn your body until your back is towards him, and place your right leg to the outside of his (Fig 224). Note that during this move, your left foot has rotated until it is parallel with the opponent's right foot.

Stiffen your right leg while turning your upper body to the left, so drawing the opponent across you. Your right hip is now under his stomach, as it was in the first hip throw and, as you draw him across your hip, so you force him to put most of his weight on his right foot. Your right leg is bent at first, with the calf pressing against the opponent's shin – well below his knee joint. This is an all-

Fig 223 **Draw the opponent strongly towards you.**

Fig 224 **Using the neck hold and forward lean, draw the opponent forward over your hip.**

important point, so be careful to get it right.

Straighten your right knee and raise your heel from the mat so the opponent's leg is lifted from the floor. Couple this with the drawing action applied by your sleeve and neck holds, so the opponent rolls over your right hip and falls on to the floor in front of you. Ensure that a straight line runs through your big toe, knee, hip, shoulder and head at the moment the throw actually occurs.

You will probably be able to throw the opponent even if your technique is poor, though you will then have to drag him across your hip, rather than simply tipping him over.

Practise ten throws, each time simply drawing your opponent forward and spinning around into the correct pre-throw position. Then concentrate on the lifting action of your right leg.

Waist Wheel

Use waist wheel in the same way as neck throw — i.e. when the opponent advances, turns or withdraws.

Take up your opening position and step across the front of the opponent's left foot with your left, turning it so the toes point at each other (Fig 225). Then step quickly around with your right foot, so it crosses both the opponent's legs. Bend your left knee as you twist around and lean to the left while straightening your right leg. Allow the heel to rise from the mat as you pull the opponent over your right thigh (Fig 226). Use both hands to help in the action, pulling strongly on his sleeve with your left hand and also drawing strongly across with your right.

Perform ten movements up to the point where you step across his legs. This will give you the feel of a correct set-up. Then perform a further ten, but this time go all the way through.

If you time things well, the opponent will be thrown cleanly and easily, and there will be no need to use great power in hauling him over. If you find the throw hard going, then keep at it until you get the timing right. Try sweeping at the opponent's leg with your left foot. This may cause

Fig 225 **Step across the front of the opponent's left foot with your left foot.**

Fig 226 **Pull the opponent over your right hip.**

him to lift his left foot, so yours passes underneath. Then spin around and throw him before he has the chance to recover his composure.

This hip throw does not use the same lifting movement which we encountered in the previous two. Here the opponent is being pivoted over his right foot – which he cannot move because you have stepped in front of it. However, you must step close across the front of him or he will be able to slide his right foot forward and reduce the unbalancing effect.

The dynamics of the throw are interesting in that you must lean away, forcing the opponent to follow suit. This is a precarious position from which the pivoting action is easily developed. Failure to tilt the opponent forwards allows him to resist your throw.

Sweeping Hip Throw

Begin from the engagement position and fit him for the throw by pulling smoothly on his sleeve while lifting his lapel. Then step in front of the opponent's feet with your left foot, turning the toes outwards. Place your foot so it is exactly mid way between the opponent's – make sure you get this right! Note that your right hip is now close to the opponent and your body is half turned away (Fig 227).

Step quickly through with your right foot, swivelling on the ball of your left. Swing your right leg back across the opponent's right thigh and, at the same time, pull on his right sleeve and push with your right. He is forced to roll over your hip and lands flat on his back on the mat (Figs 228 & 229).

You are combining the jarring action of your right leg with a pulling action to tip the opponent over. The opponent topples because his centre of gravity lies well above the barred leg.

A good idea to perfect this action is to practise the setting up sequence ten times. Then go ahead and perform ten complete throws.

Fig 227 **Step across with your left foot and turn the toes outwards.**

Fig 228 **Step quickly through with your right foot and sweep it back, bumping him into the air.**

Fig 229   Keep hold of the opponent as he is thrown to the mat in front of you.

First Shoulder Throw

Now we move away from hip throws and switch our attention instead to the first of two shoulder throws. Begin from the customary engagement position and fit the opponent by gently pulling him by his lapel, so he takes a half-step forward with his left foot.

Step across in front of his left foot with your left, so the two big toes are close together. Keep your heel off the mat so as to be able to pivot freely (Fig 230). Turn your hips to the left and step into the opponent, keeping your knees bent and your centre of gravity low. Let go of the opponent's lapel and drive your right arm up and under his. The crook in your elbow engages with his arm just above your left hand grip.

Turn your back fully on the opponent and press against his body (Fig 231). The fact that your knees are bent means that you are under his centre of gravity, and straightening them means that he is

lifted into the air. Keep your body bending forwards as you lift him, drawing on his right sleeve with your left hand while lifting him with your right. The opponent will rise up and over your back (Fig 232), dropping to the mat at your feet.

For the technique to work efficiently, you must first bend your knees, so your belt is well below his. Secondly, you must close right into him, so your back presses against his stomach. Only then is an efficient lift possible.

Train until you can run the various moves into one seamless sequence. Draw the opponent and step across in one movement, aiming to complete the turn even as weight descends upon his advancing foot. Lift the opponent's right arm by pressing upwards against his elbow and use the crook of your right elbow to take him to his toes. This will cause him stoop over you and make the lift easier. Give him no time to come to terms with what is happening before you throw him.

The throw will also work without the full fit-

Fig 230 **Step across with your left foot until the toes are close to the opponent's.**

Fig 231 **Turn your back fully on the opponent and thrust your right arm under his elbow.**

Fig 232 **The opponent rises up and over your back.**

not changed the position of your hands so your upper body is still partly turned towards the opponent. Lean to the left so your back presses firmly into the opponent's stomach. Your right elbow is now bent to a right angle. Straighten your knees to lift the opponent and draw him steadily with your grip on his sleeve. The opponent is brought to his toes and is then unbalanced over your shoulder (Fig 235), falling to his back on the mat in front of you. Keep hold of him and he will not be able to roll away.

This technique is similar to the first hip throw we looked at, except that there is no need to change the arms over first, and this can save time. Like the first hip throw, all the lifting is done by the legs – though novices generally try and lift with their right hands. This is incorrect and must be avoided. Instead, bend your knees and lower your body to the left until your right wrist feels

Fig 233 **Put your left foot slightly to the inside of the opponent's.**

ting movement. It is enough simply to lift the opponent to his toes, without also drawing him forwards.

Now try a combination throwing technique. Go for floating hip throw, aiming to slide your arm around the opponent's waist. This time, however, he spots what you are doing and obstructs your right arm. Let him think he has foiled you and switch instead to the shoulder throw position.

Second Shoulder Throw

Second shoulder throw is a technique which works well for the smaller person.

Begin from the customary start position and draw the opponent forward gently but firmly, so he advances his left leg. Then place the ball of your left foot slightly to the inside of his left foot and twist your hips to the left (Fig 233). Pivot on the ball of your left foot, bringing the right swiftly through. In doing this, your back turns to the opponent and your right foot comes to rest alongside the left, and just slightly inside the opponent's (Fig 234).

Bend your knees slightly so you drop below the opponent's centre of gravity. Note that you have

comfortable and is not bent too far.

Another word of caution is appropriate here. Second shoulder throw drops the opponent from quite a height - much higher than in the equivalent hip throw. Therefore, apply the throw gently and allow him to breakfall with his left arm upon landing.

Practise the throw ten times to the point of toppling the opponent. Then perform the technique all the way through.

PRONE DEFENSIVE POSITION

It is possible that, despite your best efforts, you fall or are thrown to the floor. If this happens, it is essential to keep the opponent in sight. Take up a prone defensive position by turning on to your left or right side and paddling yourself around using one leg. Bring your knees up to protect your

groin, and try to guard your face and head with your forearms.

Allow the opponent to come close, then lash out at his groin with your heel. Alternatively, attack his leg by hooking your instep behind his ankle while kicking hard into his kneecap (Fig 236). If you get the opportunity, fling yourself forward into his shins and bar his legs with both arms (Fig 237). This can have the effect of knocking him backwards off-balance. Continue to roll into him and attack his face with a back fist (Fig 238).

HOLDING TECHNIQUES

It may be necessary to restrain the opponent until help can arrive and if this is the case, then the following selection of restraint holds may fit the bill.

Fig 234 **Step smartly through and bend both knees.**

Fig 235 **The opponent is first lifted and then unbalanced over your shoulder.**

Fig 236 **Trap the opponent's ankle and kick out at his knee.**

Fig 237 **Bar his kick with your forearms, then roll into him.**

Fig 238 **Force him backwards off balance, then strike him with a back-fist.**

Rear Choke

Step up behind the opponent and throw your arm around his throat with the hand turned palm-downwards. Interlink your fingers, then thrust your hips forward and jam your right knee behind his, drawing him backwards and off-balance. Step back slightly to bring his head on to your shoulder and apply the strangle (Fig 239). His head is forced forward painfully by your shoulder as your wrist strangles him, and were it not for your support, he would fall backwards on to the mat. Release him the instant he claps his hands.

If you draw the opponent backwards and off-balance, then his options are reduced, though he may still think of hammering back into your groin with his fist. So turn your body slightly away from him and/or close your knees. Fail to draw him back and he will also be able to stamp on your foot, or bring the back of his head back hard into your face. The latter option is always a risk and it is why you must either always keep his head bent forwards against your shoulder, or keep your face

close to his head at all times. Try taking a big step back after securing a standing hold. This will bring him down and on to your leading knee, from where he has virtually no chance of escape (Fig 240).

Continue pulling the opponent backwards until he has to sit down with his head forced forward. Keep your feet wide apart and tighten your grip while pushing your right shoulder into the back of his head. This combination is crucial since it escalates the punishment inflicted and can be used to stop the opponent from reaching for your hair or face.

You can also drop down on to one knee behind him, but if you do, keep his head close to your face.

Apply the hold to a sitting opponent by coming up behind and throwing your arm over his shoulder. Extend your fingers and turn the palm of your hand downwards. Bar your wrist across his throat and interlink your fingers in a strong grip. Pull your elbows close to your body and push the

Fig 239 **Step back to bring his head onto your shoulder, then apply the strangle.**

Fig 240 **Bring him down onto your leading knee.**

opponent's head forwards with your right shoulder.

Imagine that he tries to escape by gathering in his legs and thrusting them out again, so that you are rolled back. Maintain the strangle while inserting your legs over his thighs and hooking your feet under his knees. Then simply lean back, force your legs straight and reapply the strangle from this new position (Fig 241).

Now I'd like to make some detailed points. The first is that when you begin to strangle the opponent, he will panic and start thrashing about. You may wish to extend your arm further across his throat, so the crook of your elbow comes to lie in front of his Adam's apple. Now, instead of drawing back and crushing his larynx, use your other hand to press in against the fist of the arm you are using to choke him. You will find that you are no longer pressing on his larynx; instead you are pressing on the carotid arteries that supply blood to the brain (Fig 242). He can still breathe and hence doesn't thrash about so violently but within 30 seconds or so, he will be unconscious.

It goes without saying that this version of the strangle is extremely dangerous when misused. Do not apply hard pressure for more than a few seconds, otherwise you will cause brain damage! The opponent must tap the mat, clap his hands or tap you to signal when he submits. Release the hold as soon as he does this.

Fig 241 **Hook both his legs with your insteps and continue to apply the strangle.**

Fig 242 **Trapping the opponent's neck in the vee of your elbow cuts off the blood supply to the brain.**

Scarf Hold

Drop on to your right knee and grip the opponent's right sleeve with your left hand. If you have previously succeeded in throwing him, then you will already be holding on to his sleeve. Throw your right arm around the back of his neck and take him by the collar (Fig 243). Move your right knee well forward and splay your legs widely for stability. Force your right arm fully under the opponent's neck until you can take hold of his jacket near to where you are gripping with your left hand. Bring your head down and to the side of his, so he is prevented from butting you in the face (Fig 244). His right arm is immobilised because you have jammed it under your left armpit.

Fig 243 Drop down onto your right knee and seize the opponent's collar and right arm.

Fig 244 Bring your head down and spread your legs wide.

Fig 245 **Push the opponent's right arm to the side.**

Fig 246 **Force his arm across his body.**

Fig 247 **Then interlink your fingers and reapply the hold.**

Shoulder Hold

If the opponent is strong, then he may succeed in freeing his right arm, in which case he may try to force your head back (Fig 245). Push his elbow with your left hand and withdraw your head, bringing his arm over your right shoulder (Fig 246). Then thrust your right arm further under his neck and interlink your fingers again. Now twist your left shoulder backwards and pull your right hand hard with the left, your head pushing against the opponent's (Fig 247).

Even if the opponent gets both arms free and thrusts them upwards, all is still not lost. Spread your legs widely and let your hands move until they are almost behind his head. Then, as he pushes your head back, lift his head and bend his neck forward by applying pressure to the back of his head. This puts great stress on the neck vertebrae and stops him pushing at your face. Make matters more difficult for him by jamming your right bicep muscle against his nose and mouth.

Cross Armlock

This hold-down technique applies leverage across a joint to hold the opponent immobile until help arrives. Use it when the opponent slips and falls, or when you have successfully thrown him to the ground. Keep your left-handed grip on the opponent's right sleeve and push the toes of your right foot under his ribs, near to his right armpit. Bend your right knee and put almost all of your weight on the right foot.

Take the opponent's wrist in your right hand and grip it firmly (Fig 248) Swing your left leg around in a circular motion that takes it around his head and across his throat (Fig 249). Lean well forward and bend your right knee so you gradually sit down, with your backside touching your right heel. Press the opponent's throat down with your left leg and twist his captured wrist so the crook of the elbow is turned upwards-facing. Lay back and draw the arm fully between your thighs. Close your thighs on his arm and raise your head to look at the opponent. Push his arm down to the right so it is flush with your right thigh (Fig 250). This extends the elbow painfully but clearly don't lever across your groin.

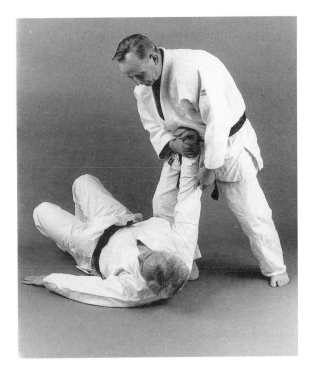

Fig 248 **Take the opponent's right wrist in your right hand.**

Fig 249 **Swing your left leg around the opponent's head and begin to sit back.**

Now I'd like to make a couple of general points. First of all, control the speed at which you sit down and lean back. Severe injury may be caused if the lock is applied and you then roll backwards too quickly. Avoid this by not pulling on the opponent's arm until you have sat down.

If you throw the opponent, then you might find that he keeps his grip on your left lapel. This makes no difference to the technique. Just lean forward and execute the roll-back, holding his wrist firmly. Because he is holding tightly to your lapel, you will be unable to lever his arm down and to the right. Instead, twist his wrist until the inside of his arm faces upwards and pin it against your chest. Grip the arm between your thighs as before, and then slowly lift your hips and thighs until he submits.

Sometimes the opponent will guess what you are doing and interlink his fingers with those of his left hand. Overcome this by swinging your left leg forwards as before but place your heel on the crook of his left elbow. Then sit down and roll

back, combining a pulling action of the hands with a pushing action of the left foot. This will generally be sufficient to break the grip.

Alternatively, shift your right hand down until it grips his sleeve near his elbow joint. Release your left hand and extend the fingers. Then press down on the opponent's throat with the edge of your hand. This will force him to release his grip in order to stop you choking him. Take advantage of this brief respite to secure the lock and roll back.

Prone Entangled Armlock

This hold-down uses leverage against the shoulder joint. Begin with the opponent lying on his back as though following a successful throw. Follow him down to the ground and push your right knee against the right side of his rib-cage. You may find that he reaches for your throat or face with his left hand and, if he does, then all well and good. Take his wrist with your left hand and rotate it until his palm faces upwards (Fig 251).

Fig 250 **Push his arm down against the top of your right thigh.**

Fig 251 **Take his wrist with your left hand.**

Fig 252 **Force his arm down to the mat, then reinforce your grip with your right arm. Press down with your left hand and lever up with your right elbow.**

Lean forwards and throw your right arm around the opponent's elbow as you push his captured arm to the floor. Press down on his chest with yours and slide your right hand forward until it is able to grasp your own left wrist. Press down with your left arm whilst levering up with the right and this will rotate his shoulder joint painfully (Fig 252).

Additional force can be applied by extending your right leg backwards and pressing down harder on his right ribs. Apply force smoothly and progressively to avoid causing unnecessary damage to the opponent's joints. You should ease up the moment he submits.

USING WRIST AND ARMLOCKS

Before going into detail about technique, I want to make a few points about the way these wrist and armlocks are applied. The first concerns the way in which they make use of the attacker's own force. The harder the attack, the more forceful the defence. Never oppose force with force, because to do so means that the stronger prevails. Instead, go with the applied force, while redirecting it to your own advantage.

Side Armlock

The attacker lunges forwards on his right foot and attempts to seize your lapel with his right hand. Draw your centre of gravity back and take his outstretched wrist in both hands. Your thumbs are applied below his palm and your fingers reach over the back of his wrist. Do not attempt to halt the attacker's thrust; let it ride upwards over your head (Fig 253).

Then swivel your hips to the right, bringing his hand down and across the front of your chest. Note how your left elbow overlaps his. Keep his arm close to your chest where you can control it, holding his palm twisted towards your chest with little finger uppermost (Fig 254).

Slide forward with your left leg and continue drawing him forward, so he is forced to take a step. Lower your left arm, trapping his extended limb beneath your armpit, then bend both your knees while pressing up against his trapped wrist. The leverage this applies to his elbow and wrist will be sufficient to hold him firmly (Fig 255).

You can release your right hand from its grip on his wrist and bring it forward to overlie your left wrist. This helps you to hold his arm more firmly against your chest and it also makes it easier to apply greater leverage (Fig 256).

Side armlock must be applied smoothly. From

Fig 253 Let the attacker's thrust ride up and past your face.

Fig 254 Swivel your hips to the right and draw out his arm, turning the hand until the little finger points upwards.

Fig 255 Bend your knees, lever down on his elbow and lift his wrist.

Fig 256 Reinforce your grip on his wrist by bringing your right arm back and pressing the trapped wrist against your chest.

the moment the attacker lunges forward to the point where he is held helpless, there is no break. The harder his attack, the quicker the technique is applied. Keep the attacker moving the whole time, so he cannot regain the advantage. Note that leverage is applied by bending the knees and, if correctly applied against a straightened arm, this will take the attacker to a face-down position on the floor. Do not allow the attacker to twist his arm around. Grip his wrist tightly and ensure that his little finger points upwards.

Arm Turn

The opponent steps forward and attempts to grab your lapel. Use his step to set yourself in motion, moving to the side with your leading foot and blocking the opponent's arm with the edge of your hand. Shoot your rear guarding hand forward and take the opponent's wrist in a firm grip (Fig 257).

Do not oppose the thrusting action, but simply lift his arm up and fold it at the elbow. You will note that in blocking towards the opponent, your

leading hand has slid over the top of the opponent's elbow, placing it in just the right position to help with the folding action (Fig 258). Bend the opponent's wrist in its natural direction, and take the trapped hand up and over his shoulder.

Curl your blocking arm around the opponent's forearm and bring it to where you are gripping his wrist. Extend your fingers and press the knife edge of your hand into the side of his bent wrist, next to where you are holding it. Then straighten both your elbows and lean forwards slightly to apply force to the trapped joint (Fig 259). If you push down into the mat, the opponent will be forced to fall diagonally backwards in front of you. Follow him down and press your knee against the side of his neck – maintaining the lock the whole time.

Entangled Armlock

The technique begins with the opponent thrusting forward on his right leg, making as though to grab your lapel with his right hand. Step forward

Fig 257 **Block with your left hand edge and seize the opponent's wrist with your right.**

Fig 258 **Use your right hand to bend the opponent's elbow across your left forearm.**

Fig 259   Drive the little finger edge of your left hand against the opponent's wrist, straighten your elbows and force him backwards.

slightly on the diagonal and fend off the arm, striking it with the edge of your left hand. Don't just knock his arm to one side; thrust your block towards the opponent's centre line.

Push his arm down and roll your left wrist under his. Take his upper arm in a firm grasp, your little finger closest to his shoulder (Fig 260). Continue moving your left arm upwards, folding it palm-upwards across your chest and jamming his wrist against your elbow. Maintain your right-handed grip on his upper arm (Fig 261). This applies a rotational pressure to the opponent's shoulder joint, forcing his head down and bringing him under control.

Three points need to be emphasized here. First of all, keep your centre line turned towards the opponent. Only then can you apply the technique efficiently. Secondly, bring your body close to the opponent in order to be able to control him effectively. Thirdly, try to judge the amount of leverage to be applied. Too much and you inflict injury. Too little and he can pull free.

It requires little effort to move the opponent's arm, because you are applying force at the wrist. Do not apply your technique higher up the forearm or it may be resisted. And don't give the opponent time to work out what is happening. You counter even as he begins to reach for your lapel; any later and the technique will not work.

The Push Down

The opponent steps forward with his right foot, thrusting his right hand forward as though to take you by the throat. Step back with your right leg and bring both hands up in front of your face, crossing them at the wrist so the palms face the opponent. This is generally known as 'cross block' though it is more of a make-safe than a block *per se* (Fig 262).

Your right hand rolls across the back of the opponent's wrist, taking it in a firm grasp and rotating it. At the same time, step around with your right foot so you are on the closed side of the opponent. Notice that your centre line continues to face him. This means you can apply force easily

Fig 260 **Lift the opponent's right arm with your left wrist whilst taking his elbow in your right hand.**

Fig 261 **Step around and lift the opponent's right arm, trapping it against your chest as you press down on his shoulder with your right hand.**

and control the opponent more effectively. Thrust the edge of your left hand forward and into the opponent's elbow joint (Fig 263).

Step further around with your right leg until you are parallel with the opponent. Bring your right arm close to your body and push down on his extended elbow joint with the edge of your left hand. His right arm is close to your left knee and all the action is near your body, where you can control him more efficiently (Fig 264).

Begin the technique even as the opponent thrusts his hand towards you. Take his arm as it is extending – not after it is at full reach. Use his movement to draw him forwards. If he has already stopped moving when you step to the side, then you will have to drag his arm out and around physically, and this makes for poor technique.

Rotate his right arm as you take it down and this will make the leverage against his elbow joint that much more effective. Finally, work close to your own body, where leverage is short and power can be directly applied.

Fig 262 **Step back and use x-block to make safe.**

Wrist Turn

The opponent lunges forward on his right foot and makes as though to grasp your lapel with his right hand. Step to the side with your leading left foot and turn your hips. Bring your left palm down and on to the back of his wrist and grasp it firmly, pressing your thumb into the back of his hand. Bring your right hand forward and reinforce the grip, so your thumbs cross over each other (Fig 265). Keep your elbows close to your sides.

Take a large sweeping step with your left leg, so your whole body turns and faces the opponent. Press with both thumbs on the back of the opponent's hand, forcing his wrist to bend in its natural direction. As you are stepping around, twist his hand until the fingers point upwards. Then press on the back of his hand until they point back to his shoulder (Fig 266). This causes severe pain and forces the opponent to roll down to the floor.

The lock is applied by the combination of stepping around and flexing the opponent's wrist so

Fig 263 **Step around and apply pressure to his extended elbow joint.**

Fig 264 **Bring his right arm close to your left knee, where you can control him.**

his fingers point towards his body. Don't be tempted to try and twist his wrist so his fingers point to the side. This takes his elbow inwards and reduces the punishment inflicted, though it may still be possible to throw him.

Once you can perform this technique, try altering the way you grip his wrist. Dig your left thumb into the back of his hand as before, but instead of following suit with your right hand, cup it over the back of the opponent's hand and attempt to roll his fingers in the direction in which they are pointing (Fig 267). This increases leverage on the wrist joint.

Fig 265 (Left) **Cross your thumbs on the back of the opponent's wrist.**

Fig 266 (Lower left) **Step sharply around with your left leg and turn the opponent's hand so the fingers point upwards.**

Fig 267 (Below) **Use the palm of your right hand to apply pressure to the back of the opponent's hand.**

Fig 268 (Above)   **Dig your thumbs into the underside of the opponent's wrist.**

Fig 269 (Above)   **Turn his hand until the little finger points upwards.**

Four-Direction Throw

The opponent steps forward with his right foot and attempts to push you in the chest. Move back slightly in order to make safe and thrust the edge of your left hand into the opponent's wrist. Don't overblock by knocking his arm outwards; simply thrust into and along his arm. Take your right arm forward with the palm facing upwards and seize hold of his wrist. Roll your left hand around and reinforce the grip so that both thumbs are pressing into the underside of his wrist (Fig 268).

Step diagonally forward with your right foot and take the opponent's hand across his body. He should not be able to resist because you are applying force at the end of his arm, where leverage is great. Turn his hand until the little finger points upwards (Fig 269).

Step through with your left foot and bend both knees to lower your height. Lift, then duck under his right arm (Fig 270), straightening up and extending your elbows (Fig 271). Pressure on his wrist forces him to the mat.

This technique requires nimble footwork and co-ordination to apply it fluidly and quickly. Any hesitation and the opponent may regain the initiative.

Wrist Twist

The opponent steps forward on his right foot and aims a punch at your face. Take a short step back to make safe, then bring both arms up and forwards in an x-block. The opponent's wrist is caught between your hand edges. Apply a double-handed grip and take the opponent's arm down and to his right. Your left hand is the lower of the two, gripping his wrist in such a way that your fingers press into his palm and your thumb is against the back of his wrist. Your right hand takes his lower forearm, just above his wrist (Fig 272). Move your body forward slightly and apply your grip through nearly straight elbows. Then step forward with your right foot, so you take his arm behind him (Fig. 273). Bend your elbows.

173

Fig 270 **Lift and duck under his right arm.**

Fig 271 **Extend your elbows and force his arm backwards.**

Turn your right foot so it points outwards, then swivel right around until you are facing in the same direction as the opponent. Once again, your elbows are nearly straight as you lift his trapped wrist high, causing his elbow to point at the ceiling. Apply a twisting action with your left hand, while lifting his arm and steadying him with the right (Fig 274). Bring his arm down, forcing him to lean forward (Fig 275), then release your right hand and step smartly around, reapplying it to his elbow (Fig 276). Draw the opponent face downwards to the mat.

This technique works if the opponent is not given time to recover after his opening punch fails. You must take his wrist even as he is punching, and draw it to the side in one seamless movement. He will not be able to resist if you time things correctly; besides which you are applying leverage to the end of his arm and this requires less effort on your part.

Fig 272 (Upper left) **Take the opponent's arm down to his right.**

Fig 273 (Upper right) **Slide your leading foot forward, taking his arm behind him.**

Fig 274 (Lower left) **Swivel right around and lift his arm whilst steadying it with your right.**

Fig 275 (Lower right) **Bring his arm down to make him lean forward.**

Fig 276   Release your right hand, step smartly around and reapply it to the opponent's elbow.

Fig 277 (Above) **Divert the opponent's attention with a vertical back-fist to the bridge of his nose.**

Fig 278 **Rotate the opponent's hand until the little finger points upwards, then press down on his bent elbow with the edge of your left hand.**

Wrist Circle

Apply wrist circle once the opponent has succeeded in taking hold of your lapel with his right hand. Don't hesitate – smack him between the eyes with a vertical back fist to divert his attention (Fig 277). Then seize his wrist with your right hand, pressing the thumb into the back of his hand and rotating it until the little finger edge is twisted upwards. At the same time, press down on his elbow joint with the edge of your left hand (Fig 278). This will drop him to his knees in front of you.

The hold works because of the 'gooseneck' shape into which you bring his arm. Make sure you are close enough to him such that both his elbow and wrist are bent. Only then will the lock work.

Some general points here: keep control over your elbows – don't let them stick out all over the place – and keep your centre line turned towards the opponent. 177

Fig 279   Grasp the opponent's wrist and elbow.

Fig 280   If the opponent resists, raise and draw back his wrist whilst bracing his elbow.

Fig 281   Bring the opponent's arm up and bend his wrist forwards.

Fig 282   Quickly slip your left arm through and reinforce your grip on the back of the opponent's hand.

Front Gooseneck

Grasp the opponent's right wrist with your right hand and take his elbow in a thumb-upwards grip (Fig 279). Stand in left posture, close to the opponent's right side, so you neither lean forward, nor overextend your arms.

If the opponent resists, apply pressure through your right hand to raise and draw back his wrist, bracing his elbow with your left hand (Fig 280). Keep the opponent's hand pointing downwards and turn it slightly outwards. Then slide your left hand under the opponent's armpit and push his forearm forward and up. Use your right hand to apply pressure to the back of his hand, so flexing the wrist (Fig 281). Quickly slide your left hand through and under the opponent's arm, joining with your right hand. By this means, the opponent's limb is trapped in the crook of your left elbow and is held there by downwards pressure applied by both of your hands to his wrist (Fig 282).

Remain close to the opponent so you can control him effectively and at the first hint of reaction against the hold, press down harder on his flexed wrist. If necessary, increase leverage by sliding your grip towards his knuckles.

12

EFFECTIVE SPARRING

INTRODUCTION

It is not my intention in this chapter simply to set down a series of sparring techniques for you to try out. Instead, I intend to discuss the tactics of fighting, because if you can understand and adopt these tactics, then you will be able to supply the appropriate techniques from your own repertoire.

All the following advice assumes that you are a reasonably competent karateka. If you are not, then read what follows for interest only and store it up until you do have the required skill!

THE THEORY BEHIND SPARRING

It does not necessarily follow that if you can fight well in the training hall, you will be able to fight well outside. This is perhaps one of the most serious mistakes made by karateka in general and leads to them making wholly false claims about their ability at self-defence.

During your training, you will spar only with other karateka, so you will become used to the way karateka attack and respond. But is it likely that the attacker you meet outsider the training hall is also a karateka and prepared to fight you according to the rules? You are much more likely to face unfamiliar Patterns of attack/response.

So, increase your versatility by sparring with students of other karate schools in order to learn how they respond. Then go beyond that and practise sparring with students of taekwondo, kung fu

and boxing, where the difference in rules is much wider than that which exists between the schools of karate and the benefit is commensurately greater.

When you spar in your club, do you envisage the possibility that the outcome may be a savage beating or possibly even death? Of course not! Yet this is precisely the case when you are forced to fight outside the club and its rules.

The presence of malice and the absence of rules leads to fear, and fear in turn inhibits the techniques which you perform so expertly in the training hall. Your muscles are slowed by fear and your strength declines. A great many martial artists become so agitated that they forget about technique altogether! Other martial artists become so aggressive that all they want to do is close with the opponent and hurt him. These aggressive martial artists also forget technique and throw caution to the four winds. In consequence they become vulnerable.

Without doubt, a calm mind is the single most important element of sparring. Even if you know only a little technique, a calm mind will ensure that you use it to best effect.

To change tack slightly, many karateka are keen to do well at sparring, but their muscles and stamina let them down. However, if you are stronger than the opponent and can maintain effective attacking pressure over a longer period, then the odds are stacked in your favour. If you can hit someone and injure them, then all other considerations become secondary.

Strength also plays an important role in protecting your internal organs from injury, because some blows at least from the opponent are going to strike home. Yet how many karateka fold up, even with a relatively light blow to the solar plexus? Such weakness could prove lethal in a true fighting situation, so it is vital to strengthen your muscles until you can take quite hard blows to the body.

Striking with power is only half of the equation; the other half consists in turning your body weapons into effective bludgeons capable of causing injury wherever they land. This does not, of course, exempt you from the need for accuracy, though it gives you a wider margin for error.

If you are weaker than the opponent, then the protection afforded by your skill looms large between you and possible defeat. There is no doubt that if you are skilful you can do much to offset a physical disadvantage by avoiding the opponent's attack while striking home with your own blows.

If you are resolved to fight – then attack the opponent before he attacks you! Why wait for him to open the attack? Why block his punch if you can beat him to the attack? I am assuming here, of course, that the opponent has given you good grounds for believing that he is about to use physical force against you. Further, I am assuming that it is not feasible for you to run away. What I do not wish to do, however, is to give you the impression that your paranoia alone is sufficient grounds for attacking harmless passers-by!

Never retire from attack, being content merely to block the opponent's hands. Take control of the situation by advancing into him. If you stay put as he squares up, then he will be able precisely to range his techniques on you. Whereas if you move into him, he may still be able to hit you, but you will have reduced the efficiency of his technique by at least a little.

Occasionally coaches advise students to look into their opponent's eyes. Yet this can daunt some people and sap their spirit. Somewhat more facetiously, one senior karateka has remarked that he knows of no case where a victim was struck by the attacker's eyeballs!

I always advise students to look at an imaginary triangle formed by the opponent's head and shoulders. This is your reference point for distance and angle. Watch this area and respond the instant you see movement there. Don't waste time thinking about what you're going to do – just do it! Your strategy is simple – to put the opponent down as quickly as possible.

My next point covers the use of multiple as opposed to single-technique responses. If you are fairly powerful, then multiple punches following each other without pause are the most effective way of bludgeoning the opponent to the floor. Keep on attacking even if one of his techniques gets through and hits you, and should one of your blows open a cut, then concentrate your efforts on widening it. I appreciate that this doesn't sound very nice, but if you are battling for your life, then your finer sensibilities must be temporarily set aside.

Someone who is bigger than you is not necessarily stronger or more resolved, but if you don't go against him strongly from the outset, then his very bulk may come to frighten you. He might have the greater strength, but your technical ability will give you the winning edge.

Don't pit your strength against his because that way leads to defeat. An opponent of equal strength has even less of an advantage, because you also have technique on your side.

What do you do when an attacker takes your most powerful punch on his vulnerable areas and is unaffected? The answer is to run away and avoid him until your training has improved! That may sound like a frivolous answer, but actually it's good advice.

Finally, I would like to make some comment as to the legality of the various strategies I have suggested. The law allows a response with such force as is necessary to nullify an attack. This is a fine rule, and should always be obeyed whenever feasible. This is of course always a decision to be made only by the individual, and it is not the intention of this book to condone violence in any, and all situations.

PREPARING TO SPAR IN THE TRAINING HALL

The best way to ease your way into free sparring is through what is called 'prearranged sparring'.

This is the exchange of agreed techniques by a pair of co-operating karateka. Typically, one will attack as the other defends/counter-attacks, but in the more sophisticated forms, the role of attacker/ defender can change during the execution of a whole series of techniques.

In its most basic form, prearranged sparring involves one attack and one response. The attacker knows exactly which techniques to use and the defender knows which responses to make. The degrees of freedom of action available to either party are therefore strictly limited. In its most advanced form, prearranged sparring has a large degree of freedom in that, while the attacker is limited to a single technique, that technique can be delivered using either the left or the right side, and the target can be anywhere on the head or body. Furthermore, the defender may use any combination of techniques to counter.

Let's begin by examining a three-step prearranged sparring sequence to see what benefits can be derived from it. Both partners face each other in fighting stances, having already decided who is to attack and who will defend. After a brief pause during which the attacker sets up range, he then steps forward and aims a single technique at the defender. The defender steps back an equal distance and attempts to guard against the technique.

The attack is repeated twice more and each time the defender steps back and guards. However, on the third response, the counter-attack is added. Then there is a brief pause as both parties withdraw simultaneously to a safe disengagement distance.

So what we have is a three-stage advance in regular cadence: one – pause – two – pause – three – counter-attack – withdraw. There are no feints or diversionary moves. When the attacker begins, the defender knows what is coming, where it's aimed at and what he must do to avoid it. In such a controlled environment, the risk of injury is low and the defender can concentrate on good technique, fluid movement, correct distancing and good timing.

The attacker always advances a certain amount each time and the defender withdraws by a similar distance. If he withdraws too far, then there will be no need to guard and no possibility of an immediate counter-attack. But if he doesn't withdraw

far enough, then the attacker will overstep him, treading on toes and making the counter-attack difficult to use because of the unexpectedly close range. The series of steps gives practice in maintaining distance through several moves – not just one – so five-step sparring is probably even better in this respect!

The three-step sequence also teaches timing of the response, so it doesn't happen too early or too late. Typically, novices respond too slowly and the attack has reached them before they have stepped back far enough.

The trick is always to get the partners to co-operate. Aggressive attackers advance too quickly for the skill level of their partners, with the result that they overwhelm the defence. Also, aggressive defenders really belt the attacker's arm as they block it, and dig their counter-punches deep into his ribs. Nothing is more calculated to ruin the benefits of prearranged sparring than that!

One-step prearranged sparring should be a step towards realism, with everything done as realistically as possible. In its most advanced form, your partner can use any version of a particular technique, while you respond in any way that proves successful. Even so, you only have to deal with one attacking technique, so you needn't feel under too great a pressure.

This is how prearranged sparring can teach fairly basic principles and, at the same time, provide a phased introduction to the rigours of actual free sparring. All novices should proceed through three, five and one-step sequences before trying the real thing.

FREE SPARRING IN THE TRAINING HALL

Do not begin to free spar until you have practised prearranged sparring and can perform combination techniques accurately and with control. Free sparring too early in your training inevitably leads to disappointment when the techniques that work so well against the bag and target mitt fail against a partner who strikes back. There is also the question of injury. Statistics from the Martial Arts Commission prove that free sparring by relatively unskilled performers is risky.

Before free sparring, there is the question of padding to be considered. Some people believe this is essential to limit the inevitable bruising. Others think that you come to rely upon it and fail to control your techniques properly. But most people agree with the notion of using defensive padding.

The punching mitt you select must not enclose your thumb because experience has shown that this prevents you from forming a proper fist – and this in turn can lead to injury. Shin pads are useful and many people prefer those which extend down into an instep protector. Female karateka may choose to wear a breast shield, or a padded jacket of the type used in the World Taekwondo Federation. Boxing-type groin guards are reckoned to give good protection, but don't use the plastic cups which simply slip into a jock strap. A properly fitted gumshield is essential for protecting your teeth.

Don't wear spectacles or hard contact lenses for sparring. Also remove earrings, watches, necklaces and rings. Long hair should be held back with an elastic band and all hard plastic or metal grips must be removed. Keep finger and toenails clean and short.

During sparring, you may come into close contact with the opponent. Therefore make sure that your personal hygiene is all that it ought to be.

Start off by sparring with someone you can trust – preferably someone of equal mass, reach and skill. Begin sparring at a slower than normal speed, but do not take advantage of this to seize hold of slow-moving kicks. Try to dominate the opponent by using range, distance and line to your advantage.

Pace your free sparring and stop as soon as you begin to tire, because skill levels drop and mistakes increase as tiredness creeps in.

Practise with as many different people as you can, and when your skill and confidence allows, increase speed until you are both moving nearly flat-out. But always control your techniques for the sake of your partner, and avoid snarl-ups by disengaging and nodding each time either of you scores a clear and effective hit on the other. Without this, sparring just degenerates into a melee of arms and legs.

This is particularly important if you go down into ground work following a throw or fall. If you can't pinion the opponent in 10 seconds, release and try again from the standing position.

Appendix A

A FREESTYLE GRADING SYLLABUS

INTRODUCTION

The following syllabus is offered as food for thought. It sets out a ladder of progression which will take the novice through to black belt in a total of 420 hours' training. The best length (in terms of skill uptake) for a karate lesson is 90 minutes, so the above figure translates out as 280 training sessions. At two sessions per week, the average time taken will be just over $2\frac{1}{2}$ years.

RED BELT TO WHITE BELT

Grading requirement: minimum 24 hours training.

Student must be able to demonstrate a satisfactory impact against a pad with all punching, striking and kicking techniques.

Punches

From stationary fighting stance:

1 snap punch
2 reverse punch
3 hooking punch
4 close punch
5 snap punch/reverse punch.

Strikes

Student must show how the following strikes are applied, and to which targets:

1 hammer-fist (two versions)

2 back-fist (two versions)
3 One-knuckle punch (two versions)

Kicks

From fighting stance:

1 front kick
2 roundhouse kick
3 front kick/roundhouse kick/reverse punch.

Single kicks must be above the waist.

Blocks

Student must show how the following blocks are applied to a stationary outstretched arm, and be able to explain the difference between the opponent's open and closed sides:

1 head block
2 rising block.

Each block must be performed in conjunction with a counter-attack consisting of a punch or strike taken from this syllabus.

Throwing Techniques

1 Back breakfall from standing position.
2 Side breakfall from standing position.

WHITE BELT TO YELLOW BELT

Grading requirement: minimum 36 hours' training since last grading.

Punches

Delivered while stepping forward or backwards:

1 snap punch
2 reverse punch
3 snap punch/reverse punch
4 reverse punch/reverse punch.

Strikes

Strikes must show application against target:

1 knife-hand (two versions)
2 palm-heel (two versions).

Kicks

Delivered from a fighting stance or straddle stance:

1 side kick
2 back kick
3 roundhouse kick/back kick/reverse punch
4 side kick/back kick/reverse punch.

Single kicks must be above waist height.

Blocks

Blocks must be shown correctly against a stationary and outstretched arm. Student must be able to show the difference between blocking to opponent's closed side and blocking to his open side.

1 inner forearm block
2 outer forearm block.

Both of these blocks must be performed together with an appropriate punch or strike.

Throwing Techniques

1 Front breakfall from standing position.
2 Rolling front breakfall from standing position.

Holding Techniques

1 Rear choke.
2 Scarf hold.

Locking Techniques

Applied to a moving but outstretched arm:

1 side armlock
2 arm turn.

Sparring

The student must be able to show control of distance and timing by means of simple three or five-step routines in which the opponent advances and the defender steps back.

YELLOW BELT TO ORANGE BELT

Grading requirement: minimum 48 hours' training since last grading.

Punches

Delivered while sliding and stepping forward or stepping backwards:

1 hip twist snap punch
2 reverse punch
3 hip twist snap punch/reverse punch
4 front kick/hip twist snap punch/reverse punch/roundhouse kick.

Strikes

Strikes must show application against target:

1 Ridge-hand
2 Spear-hand (three versions).

Kicks

Delivered from a fighting stance or straddle stance:

1 one-step front kick
2 skipping front kick
3 one-step roundhouse kick

4   skipping roundhouse kick
5   skipping front kick/snap punch
6   skipping roundhouse kick/reverse punch.

Single kicks must be above the waist.

Blocks

Blocks must be shown correctly against a stationary and outstretched arm. Student must be able to show the difference between blocking to opponent's closed side and blocking to his open side.

1   knife block (two versions)
2   palm-heel block (two versions).

An appropriate strike or punch must be applied following each block.

Throwing Techniques

1   Leg throw
2   Floating hip.

Holding Techniques

1   Shoulder hold
2   Cross armlock.

Locking Techniques

Applied to a moving outstretched arm:

1   entangled armlock,
2   push down.

Sparring

The student must use three or five-step sparring to demonstrate his ability at timing and distance. An effective counter-attack must be delivered at the conclusion of each sequence.

Slowed-down free sparring may be allowed.

ORANGE BELT TO GREEN BELT

Grading requirement: minimum 48 hours' training after previous grading.

Punches

Student must show how to change line so as to be able to punch from an advantageous position. Punches are delivered in the form of sequences while sliding and stepping forward and while advancing on the diagonals. They must also be delivered while stepping or sliding back on the diagonals.

The student must be able to generate sufficient force in short-distance punches on both hands.

All punches must be shown against an opponent using target mitts.

Strikes

Strikes must show application against target:

1   elbow (four versions).

Kicks

Delivered from a fighting stance or straddle stance:

1   one-step side kick
2   skipping side kick
3   one-step back kick
4   180° reverse roundhouse kick
5   front foot roundhouse kick to head
6   side kick with the rear leg.

All kicks must be above waist height.

Blocks

Blocks must be shown correctly against a stationary and outstretched arm, with the exception of scooping block, which must be shown against a front kick. Students must be able to show the difference between blocking to opponent's closed side and blocking to his open side:

1   lower parry
2   scooping block against a front kick
3   double blocks numbers one and two.

Each block must be shown in conjunction with a valid punch or strike.

Throwing Techniques

1 Neck throw.
2 Waist wheel.

Holding Techniques

1 Prone entangled armlock.

Locking Techniques

Applied to a moving outstretched arm:

1 wrist turn
2 four-direction throw.

Sparring

The student must now be able to demonstrate at least four one-step sparring routines in which a realistic attack is countered by an effective defence. One of these routines must include a sweeping or hooking technique.

At least 2 minutes of effective free sparring is required for the grading.

GREEN BELT TO PURPLE BELT

Grading requirement: minimum 48 hours' training after previous grading.

Punches

Student must show how to control distance, change line and punch while on the move from any position. The examiner can ask for any combination of punches delivered in any particular mode.

The student must be able to demonstrate effective close-range punches delivered while on the move, and while changing line.

These techniques must be shown against an opponent who has either target mitts or an impact pad.

Strikes

The student must select and demonstrate the use of four strikes from close distance as part of a pre-arranged sparring routine.

Kicks

Delivered from a fighting stance:

1 Axe kick
2 Inner and outer crescent kicks
3 One-step 180° reverse roundhouse kick
4 180° reverse crescent kick.

All kicks must be to head height.

Blocks

Blocks must be shown correctly against a stationary and outstretched arm. Student must be able to show the difference between blocking to opponent's closed side and blocking to his open side:

1 Hooking block alone
2 Hooking block used after another block to close off opponent.

Throwing Techniques

1 Sweeping hip.
2 Shoulder throws numbers one and two.

Holding Techniques

The examiner may ask for any hold to be demonstrated.

Locking Techniques

Applied to moving outstretched arm:

1 Wrist twist
2 Wrist turn
3 Front gooseneck.

Sparring

Student must select and show at least six one-step sparring routines which satisfy the criteria for effective application. Two of these routines must include a foot sweep or hooking sequence.

In addition, the student must demonstrate an adequate standard of free sparring for at least 3 minutes.

PURPLE BELT TO BLUE BELT

Grading requirement: minimum 48 hours' training after previous grading.

Punches

Student must show how to control distance, change line and punch while on the move from any position. The examiner can ask for any combination of punches delivered in any particular mode.

The student must be able to demonstrate effective close range punches delivered while on the move and while changing line.

These techniques must be shown against an opponent who has either target mitts or an impact pad.

Strikes

The student must select and demonstrate the use of six strikes from close distance as part of a prearranged sparring routine.

Kicks

The student must be able to demonstrate any kick or combination of kicks that the examiner requires. Students must be able to demonstrate multiple kicks on one leg, without setting the foot down between successive deliveries.

Blocks

The student must select and demonstrate four blocks against a prearranged attack.

Throwing Techniques

The examiner can ask for any throw to be performed on either the left or right sides.

Holding Techniques

The examiner can ask for any hold to be demonstrated. The student must also show how the hold can be maintained against resistance from the partner.

Locking Techniques

The examiner can ask for any locking technique to be demonstrated on either the left or the right sides.

Sparring

Student must select and show at least six one-step sparring routines which satisfy the criteria for effective application. Two of these routines must include foot sweeps or hooks.

In addition, the student must demonstrate an adequate standard of free sparring for at least two bouts, each of which lasts 3 minutes

BLUE BELT TO BROWN BELT

Grading requirement: minimum 72 hours, training after previous grading.

Punches

Student must show ability at controlling distance, changing line and punching while on the move and from any position. The examiner can ask for any combination of punches delivered in any particular mode.

The student must be able to demonstrate effective close range punches delivered while on the move, and while changing line.

These techniques must be shown against an opponent who has either target mitts or an impact pad.

Strikes

Student must show ability at controlling distance, changing line and striking while on the move and from any position. The examiner can ask for any combination of strikes delivered in any particular mode.

The student must be able to demonstrate effective close range strikes delivered while on the move and while changing line.

These techniques must be shown against an opponent who has either target mitts or an impact pad.

Kicks

The student must be able to demonstrate any kick or combination of kicks that the examiner requires. Students must be able to demonstrate multiple kicks on one leg, without setting the foot down between successive deliveries.

The examiner may also request any combination of kicks, strikes, blocks and punches to be performed.

Blocks

The student must select and demonstrate four blocks against a prearranged attack.

Throwing Techniques

The examiner can ask for any throw to be performed on either the left or right sides.

Holding Techniques

The examiner can ask for any hold to be demonstrated. The student must also show how the hold can be maintained against resistance from the partner.

Locking Techniques

The examiner can ask for any locking technique to be demonstrated on either the left or the right sides.

Sparring

Student must select and show at least six one-step sparring routines which satisfy the criteria for effective application. Two of these routines must include foot sweeps or hooks.

In addition, the student must demonstrate an adequate standard of free sparring for at least two bouts, each of which lasts 3 minutes.

BROWN BELT TO BLACK BELT

Grading requirements: minimum 96 hours' training after previous grading and student must hold at least a National Coaching Foundation Level One coaching qualification.

Punches

Student must show ability at controlling distance, changing line and punching hard while on the move and from any position. The examiner can ask for any combination of punches delivered in any particular mode.

The student must be able to demonstrate effective close range punches delivered while on the move, and while changing line.

These techniques must be shown against an opponent who has either target mitts or an impact pad.

Strikes

Student must show ability at controlling distance, changing line and striking hard while on the move and from any position. The examiner can ask for any combination of strikes delivered in any particular mode.

The student must be able to demonstrate effective close range strikes delivered while on the move and while changing line.

These techniques must be shown against an opponent who has either target mitts or an impact pad.

Kicks

The student must be able to demonstrate any kick or combination of kicks that the examiner requires. Students must be able to demonstrate multiple kicks on one leg, without setting the foot down between successive deliveries.

The examiner may also request any combination of kicks, strikes, blocks and punches to be performed.

Blocks

The student must select and demonstrate four blocks against a prearranged attack.

Throwing Techniques

The examiner can ask for any throw to be performed on either the left or right sides.

Holding Techniques

The examiner can ask for any hold to be demonstrated. The student must also show how the hold can be maintained against resistance from the partner.

Locking Techniques

The examiner can ask for any locking technique to be demonstrated on either the left or the right sides.

Sparring

Student must select and show at least six one-step sparring routines which satisfy the criteria for effective application. Two of these routines must include foot sweeps or hooks.

In addition, the student must demonstrate an adequate standard of free sparring for at least two bouts, each of which lasts 3 minutes. The student must then spar with two lower grade students simultaneously for up to 1 minute.